FROM THE HAPPY SHEET TO THE BOTTOM LINE

Solving the Return on Investment Challenge

Patrick Taggart (MA HRM) and Gail Sheppard (MBA)

First published in Great Britain in 2010
by GPSVision Ltd
The TechnoCentre, Puma Way, Coventry, CV1 2TT

ISBN 978-0-9564901-0-0

Printed in Great Britain by Rubicon Corporate Print Limited
Cover design by Amy Chubb

CONTENTS

Table of figures

ABOUT THE AUTHORS

Patrick Taggart MA (HRM), Chartered FCIPD

Patrick has worked in senior management positions in the distribution and financial services sectors. In the 1990s Patrick became an independent HRM consultant. However his dissertation on 'Management development in professional football' developed his interest in the complex field of development and ROI.

Gail Sheppard BSc (Hons), CSS, MBA, PGC(HE)

Gail worked as a Senior Manager in Local Government until the late 1990s, at which time she left the public sector to become an independent organisational development consultant. She developed a particular interest in organisational culture and change, following her dissertation 'Language and culture: barriers to collaboration between Social Services and Health'.

Patrick and Gail met whilst working as Senior Lecturers at Coventry University in Business and Management development, including managing a European funded project, known as the Skills Jigsaw, which delivered management development to over 200 West Midlands based organisations. This work engendered their interest in measuring and evaluating the impact of development activity. They decided to leave the University to develop systems that would help organisations to improve and measure the impact from their learning and development activities. They bring years of experience to the subject of Return on Investment and help their customers to challenge the status quo around a flawed and faith based approach that has existed for too long around learning and development.

ACKNOWLEDGEMENTS

Thanks to the following who offered invaluable help in this project:

Dave McCabe and Christine Fiddis for assisting in the drafting of the book

Philip Crisp, Geraldine Taggart and Judy Ryder for proof reading and constructive feedback

Lesley Marriott for case study design and data management

Clare Schofield for cover design and publishing support

Toby Whiteley for support and advice on layout and publishing

Pratik Sheth for Internship contribution

All our customers for being open to a new approach to L&D

PREFACE

Most organisations have an annual budget for Training and Staff Development, managed by Human Resources or Learning and Development specialists, and it is used to deliver a range of different training initiatives. This budget is often reduced or removed in difficult times as organisations are unable to show a positive Return on Investment (ROI) to the organisation. Applying the process set out in this book will mean the reader is able to prove a positive ROI to their organisation and thus be well prepared should they need to make a case for continuing to invest in their staff.

Currently most organisations have inadequate processes in place to show ROI, which is an unacceptable position in today's cost conscious climate. This book sets out to help the reader address this situation. It will teach the reader how to demonstrate ROI and produce reports showing the effect on the bottom line for circulation to the relevant stakeholders.

So why does return on investment continue to be such a challenge for organisations and learning and development professionals? Our work as Learning and Development Consultants made us recognise that the primary tool for evaluating training processes is the end-of-course ritual fondly known as the "happy sheet". Coming in a variety of shapes and sizes, this is the final act of most training sessions. For many course participants, this was the end of the process for them, too. Generally, there was no attention paid to what they had learned, if they changed their behaviour, applied new skills and whether this made a difference to them, their team, their work or added value to the organisation and customers! See our website www.gpsvision.co.uk for Patrick's presentation on how organisations can move quickly from a dependence on the happy sheet.

Whilst the training process and content may be relevant, enjoyable and interesting, we believe that a more holistic approach to learning is required to ensure that it is transferred and 'embedded' into the workplace. Only by taking this approach will organisations know that their investment in learning is directly improving the performance of their organisation and a positive return on investment achieved.

Research carried out by the American Society of Training and Development[i] showed only 4% of organisations were evaluating learning at the bottom line level. This is a missed opportunity and lacks the accountability required in today's cost conscious climate. Research carried out by Saratoga/PWC[ii] in 2005 showed that over £1 billion was spent on leadership training across Europe, yet they could find little evidence of any major return. This research supports our view that organisations take unacceptable risks with their learning and development budgets and possibly hope things will work, rather than invest a little more time in ensuring they work.

In talking to Learning and Development Professionals, it is clear that most investment in training and development is faith based, not evidence based. Little wonder that Finance Directors sometimes question the effectiveness of training when the professionals themselves find it difficult to demonstrate. This is an unacceptable predicament and we have spent many years developing a system that helps professionals to demonstrate ROI and report on the effectiveness of their learning initiatives. We have proven that our methodology can shift learning and development from a faith based approach to an evidence based approach.

Our system is called the Performance Improvement Cycle©, which is a holistic methodology to improve and to measure learning outcomes. This methodology has already saved clients thousands of pounds by focusing development effort on the before, during and after phases of development initiatives. The PIC© process has been applied to over fifty organisations, delivering excellent results, some of which are set out in the following case studies. Three recent customers invested £50,000 and made savings to the value of £300,000. Would your organisation reduce its training budget if presented with these results?

Our PIC© is a practical and useable process and we have proven that it can be applied across a broad range of development initiatives and sectors.

This book explores a different approach to organisational learning that challenges the status quo. The case studies illustrate how GPSVision is changing organisational learning through using their Performance Improvement Cycle©. It also provides tips and suggestions showing how by changing your approach, organisations can develop a Return on Investment culture by educating their managers and leaders to support ROI. In this group of case studies we have focused particularly on Return on Investment from Leadership and Management Development. We recognise that it is not as easy as some more quantifiable spheres of development; however our case studies show that although challenging, it is possible.

Our target audience

This book will be of great value to anyone who is involved in improving the performance of their organisation through the delivery of better learning interventions. Traditionally this has been the role of Human Resource or Learning and Development professionals, but increasingly all who have a stake in the organisation's performance could benefit. Ultimately it is the responsibility of all employees that learning and development should add value and we have learned that the more stakeholders there are looking for a positive ROI, the easier it is to achieve. Irrespective of the type of business or sector, we know that all organisations can benefit from our approach, which puts organisational improvement at the heart of development initiatives.

Future development

To make managing ROI even easier for organisations we have spent two years developing a software solution to help in this quest. Odissy ™ is an innovative, online system that revolutionises the learning and development process and helps customers to efficiently apply the Performance Improvement Cycle© to all development initiatives. It aligns employee and organisational objectives thereby improving the focus on organisational performance, automates the project management challenges of development interventions, supports the employees' learning experience, enhances the learning transfer processes and automates a range of ROI reports for circulation to key stakeholders. These can also be used for submissions for national training awards. This is explained in more detail in Chapter 12.

Patrick Taggart and Gail Sheppard

March 2010

CHAPTER I

THE CHALLENGES OF DELIVERING RETURN ON INVESTMENT

> *It is to the great shame of the training 'profession' that it has failed to produce a universally accepted and workable evaluation methodology.*
>
> (Paul Kearns 2005)[iii]

A hard-hitting, but arguably fair statement about the inadequate approach to evaluation that exists in most organisations today. Our work at GPSVision has been helping our customers to successfully address this problem.

The Challenge

Developing employee skills across all levels of an organisation is increasingly recognised as critical to sustainable success. Developing employees is therefore vital to future competitiveness and innovation. Organisations are changing from hierarchical corporate structures, where decision-making is focused at board level, to flatter structures. This leads to more devolved decision making at all levels from middle and junior management, team leaders and individual employees. This is generating the need for better leadership and management skills across organisations.

Leadership and management development is already recognised by many organisations as a high priority for investment. However, although organisations are increasingly focusing time and money on developing their talent pool of present and future leaders, there is limited evidence of quantifiable payback and bottom line improvement. Ongoing investment continues to be a leap of faith.

> *Most organisations are concerned with some form of measure of return on investment (ROI), but not many maintain records or IT systems that would give them data to measure any returns.*
>
> (CMI 2007)[iv]

> *Organisations across Europe spent £1.03 billion on leadership training in 2003 with little evidence of major return.*
>
> (Saratoga/Price Waterhouse Coopers 2005)[v]

Learning and Development professionals struggle to justify the ongoing cost of employee development often due to their inability to demonstrate a positive ROI. There is an increasing trend to recruit leaders externally, which may be the result of poor investment, or the cause of it. Research shows that only 21% of UK leaders are appointed from within the organisation, compared to 37% of overseas companies (DDI 2005)[vi] This trend is particularly prevalent in the public sector where 3 in 4 employers prefer to recruit, rather than develop their own people.

The Missing Link

Ensuring that investment in employee development is translated into bottom line performance is a key challenge for the 21st century organisation. It is also the ultimate source of future competitive advantage and innovation. Unfortunately this is also a major area of weakness for many organisations where there is a process gap or missing link between spend on employee development and the ability to demonstrate quantifiable outcomes.

This lack of a proven methodology or process is a major barrier to demonstrating outcomes. The majority of initiatives that have looked at this issue have examined individual areas of delivery, rather than the need for a total change in approach, which is required.

The result is that employee development often results in a disappointing outcome. The symptoms of this can be:

- Embedded behaviour change is frequently not achieved, with training being seen as a one off event.

- No effective measurement systems are established to track outcomes, so it remains unclear whether the investment has added value to the individual, team, organisation or customer.
- The infrastructure to support knowledge acquisition, application and dissemination is frequently lacking in organisations, either through a haphazard approach to knowledge management, or where the culture allows a few individuals to use knowledge as a power base. Learning may be viewed as a means of personal progression rather than a shared resource.

Paradigm Shift or Gradual Illumination

Early in our research and development we produced a White Paper (GPSVision 2005)[vii]. We were frustrated by the current situation, hence the wish for a paradigm shift, or fundamental and revolutionary change. However, experience has shown us that this change is more likely to be achieved through an evolutionary process. Much of this change must be led by champions, those who are passionate about the value of development activities and how they can be of demonstrable benefit to the organisation.

This change in approach is not complicated, but does require the development of a sound framework which can be applied consistently around development initiatives. The methodology which we have used with our customers includes:

- A clear understanding of an organisation's needs
- Individual learner's current knowledge and skills
- Setting specific outputs that include potential cost reductions or revenue increases
- A support strategy to embed any learning into the workplace
- An effective measurement system
- A return on investment (ROI) reporting process

At GPSVision, we have proved that our methodology helps organisations to improve their performance through effective employee development that can be tracked to the bottom line. However despite our valiant efforts the following two quotes show the plight that organisations face around managing ROI. UK organisations are poor at managing ROI and there is still much to do to get the majority of organisations managing ROI effectively.

> *UK organisations are particularly remiss in areas such as not holding senior managers accountable for leadership development, being inconsistent in the way they deploy programmes across locations, and failing to measure the results of leadership development*
>
> DDI Survey Report 2008 [viii]
>
> *ROI is alive and well as a tool for measuring the success of learning and development. Almost 4000 organisations are using ROI around the world*
>
> Knowledge Advisors 2009[ix]

CHAPTER 2

OUR RESEARCH AND LEARNING

To pursue our quest of making return on investment a manageable task for customers, we researched other writers and specialists on the subject. Our first influence was Kirkpatrick (1994)[x]. He described how, when evaluating a training activity, an assessment should be made at four levels:

- Level 1 involves assessing learner's reactions to the activity. Relatively simple and cheap to assess (usually in the form of evaluation questionnaires or feedback forms)
- Level 2 assesses what learners have learned (in terms of knowledge, skills and/or attitude) as a result of participating in the activity.
- Level 3 investigates behavioural changes, or the extent to which the learner has applied the newly acquired learning in the workplace.
- Level 4 assesses the benefits of training at an organisational level rather than an individual level, presented in terms of bottom line benefits easily recognisable to senior management.

The model gradually shifts in focus from the learner (Levels 1 and 2) to the organisation (Levels 3 and 4). As they are the most difficult and time-consuming to conduct, the latter levels are often neglected. Yet these are the levels that yield the most valuable data and can provide a thorough justification for future training expenditure.

Jack Phillips (2003) [xi] approach to the evaluation of learning activities builds on the work of Kirkpatrick, whom he openly credits with ideas for developing the first four levels of his own framework for evaluation. The significant difference is that Phillips has renamed the first four levels, and has added a fifth to capture return on investment.

- Level 1 Reaction, satisfaction and planned action: measures the extent to which the participants enjoyed the learning experience and establishes how they plan to apply their learning.
- Level 2 Learning: measures the extent to which the participants have increased their knowledge and improved their skill levels.
- Level 3 Application and implementation: measures the extent to which the participants have applied what they learned from the learning event to their working practice.
- Level 4 Business impact: measures the results that the participants have achieved as a result of applying what they learned from the learning event. This would include measures such as output, quality, cost, time, customer satisfaction and employee satisfaction.
- Level 5 Return on investment: measures the level of monetary benefit against the overall cost of the learning event and then compares the two. Usually expressed as a percentage or cost benefit ratio.

John Darling (2006) [xii] developed the concept of embedding learning as an important phase of learning, suggesting that the better distribution of attention in the process moves from the actual training event to both the "before" and "after" phase. He showed the traditional models as seeing the training as the cornerstone of the process, whereas his model shows it as just another phase in several required phases.

Figure 1 John Darling: Embedding Learning

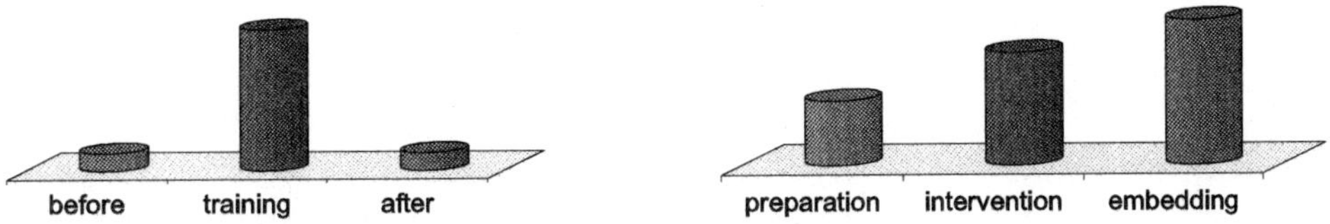

Dr. Elwood (Ed) Holton (2000) [xiii] has written extensively on the factors affecting the transfer of learning as a result of training activities, and has developed a practical model called the Learning Transfer System Inventory. This model identifies a number of potential enhancers or barriers to the practical application of learning, which include motivation, environment, ability and readiness. This model showed us that the transfer climate was a factor that was often missing from learning initiatives which, if not addressed, would significantly affect the results. Learning transfer has become a key phase in our PIC© and a very important part of the holistic process.

Paul Kearns (2005)[xiv] in his book Evaluating the ROI from Learning, has identified the optimum way to measure value from development activities on the basis of his three box system, with the middle box - value added training - as an area in which organisations should be pursuing the actual value. However, he puts much of the soft skills development, such as leadership and management development, into the box "nice to have" and showed how this area of development could be measured if evaluated in a more systematic manner.

These are some of the key influencers to our work and this learning helped us to develop the Performance Improvement Cycle© as described in the next Chapter.

CHAPTER 3

THE PERFORMANCE IMPROVEMENT CYCLE©

Great leadership is not measured merely by the success of a business at a single point in time. The test is in building an organisation that is adaptive, resilient and ready for the challenges of tomorrow

(Bennis 2005)[xv]

Any organisation investing in traditional training programmes can currently expect to see only a minimal return on their investment - if they can measure it at all. A change in approach to learning and development is required if organisations are to obtain improved bottom line performance.

The Performance Improvement Cycle© was developed by GPSVision, as a result of our experience, observation and research (See Chapter 2). We recognised that participants in leadership and management programmes were struggling to apply their learning, and organisations were unable to produce meaningful return on investment data. The main reason for this was a failure to incorporate programme content into part of a broader system or process of learning. Typically this failure resulted from:

- No tangible outcomes specified at the beginning of the process
- Lack of ownership and support by senior and line managers
- Training evaluation rarely going beyond the reaction level
- No reflective learning or action planning processes in place to help individuals to apply new skills in the work place

The Performance Improvement Cycle© supports companies in making the change needed in their approach to organisational development. By adopting this methodology, organisations are able to develop an effective link between strategy and implementation. This enables embedded behaviour change and real performance improvement in bottom line performance. (See Figure 2)

Figure 2 Moving from the traditional approach to the PIC© approach to organisational development

Traditional approach to organisational development	PIC© approach to organisational development
Managers seen as talent users	Managers seen as talent developers
Knowledge is compartmentalised Focus on individual knowledge Knowledge is power culture	Knowledge is shared Focus on knowledge transfer and collaboration between individuals
Large scale training programmes Focus on the classroom Unrealistic expectations of formal training programmes	Customised approach to organisational development, self driven content, coaching and mentoring, group focus and action learning support
One off training programmes leading to a transient effect	Long term commitment to organisational development giving embedded behaviour change
Happy sheets, basic measurements	Meaningful and relevant measurement at several levels
Focus on content and classroom	Focus on bottom line improvement, hard benefits and behaviour change
Learning is seen as a tactical solution to a requirement	Learning is seen as critical to strategy implementation and an ongoing process

Source: GPSVision (2005)[xvi]

Creating a holistic approach to Organisational Development

The Performance Improvement Cycle© is a methodology that not only measures and evaluates, but increases the return on investment from development activities. One of the key objectives of the system is to enable a change in the learning culture, rather than measure one off events in reaction to a particular business issue, or individual development requirement. This means that individuals, organisations and customers all benefit from PIC© and the enhanced bottom line results provided by the approach.

The PIC© System consists of a six stage continuous process which can be applied to all learning processes including the softer skills areas that are required at all levels across an organisation such as leadership, management, personal effectiveness and customer facing activities.

Figure 3 The Performance Improvement Cycle© (PIC ©)

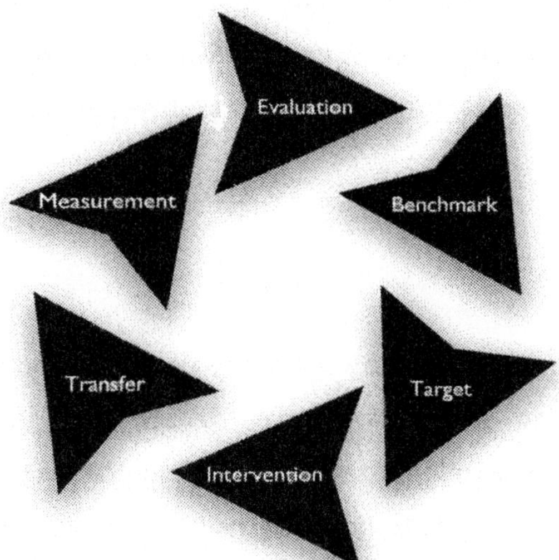

Evaluation

Most organisations believe that evaluation completes their learning interventions. However this is why they find evaluation and ROI difficult. Evaluation must take place before any learning intervention is implemented. The process must begin and end with an evaluation phase. An evaluation is carried out on the main performance indicators of the organisation which include financial, employee, customer satisfaction and productivity data. This data highlights areas for improvement within the organisation; these generally lead to Key Performance Indicators (KPIs), external and/or internal data. It is also very important to agree the milestones for the evaluation process and how and when evaluation data will be collected and shared with relevant stakeholders, including participants, line managers, L&D specialists and executives.

Benchmark

Once the evaluation phase has identified development needs, the benchmarking phase provides data on the skills/experience levels of employees who could address these needs. This can be done at an individual or team level. This can involve various diagnostics, such as 360° skill evaluations and team performance audits. Organisations may have performance appraisal data that may help at this stage. In order to assess personal improvement it is essential that the organisation has a clear picture of where employees are starting from.

Targets

The data collected will lead to targets for improvement. These can be at organisational, team/individual and customer level. These can include targets that when achieved will deliver a monetary return to the organisation in terms of savings or increased revenue and/or some that are less tangible. These targets become the key drivers for the development intervention and need to be clearly communicated to all involved in the intervention. This approach raises the expectations of all stakeholders and the improvement based focus of the intervention. It also highlights the need for all to support and engage in the evaluation process.

Intervention

An intervention is whatever it takes to help the organisation achieve the targets identified during the evaluation, benchmarking and target setting phases. It can be formal or informal and needs to be aligned with the organisation's culture and fit the learning preferences of the staff involved. Most employees see the intervention as the cornerstone of the learning process and they need to be made aware that it is only peripheral to the process. Organisations have been negligent at addressing this misunderstanding, which it has perpetuated by not expecting a ROI from the intervention. It is not surprising that employees think learning is about personal improvement if the organisation does not look for its own ROI. Our approach has helped employees to think both personal improvement and the bottom line at the same time.

Transfer

Learning transfer is a critical aspect of ensuring post intervention activity can achieve the agreed targets. This stage is essential to ensure that new learning is embedded into the organisation and is perhaps the most common omission within current learning initiatives. Employees often complain that they were not given opportunities to apply their new skills and knowledge. Effective learning transfer strategies include:

- formal assessments
- coaching and mentoring support
- action learning sets
- goal setting and reflective practice
- project implementation
- line managers providing helpful pre- and post-intervention support

Our experience shows this area is more successful if the organisation has a strong champion who keeps an active interest in all L&D activities.

Measurement

Outcomes are measured throughout the development process. This will include level one evaluation to assess reaction levels to formal interventions. Learning can often be assessed shortly after the intervention by questionnaires or if it is an accredited process at an agreed time after the intervention. Behavioural change and skills application evidence is collected between three and twelve months after the intervention. The impact on the individual, team, organisation and customer and ROI results are collected and collated between six and twelve months after the final intervention. The results will show the performance against the original targets and data is collected using a variety of methods that may include self-assessment, peer assessment, 360° assessment, workflow improvements, customer satisfaction results, productivity assessment, goal achievement and project outcomes.

Evaluation

You end by asking "have we arrived?" Having completed the measurement section the organisation can now review the entire process. Return on Investment reports can be produced and presented to key stakeholders and circulated across the organisation. Circulating the results to participants also serves to reinforce the need for effective evaluation and completes the loop for those engaging in the evaluation process. The results will help the organisation to make decisions on future initiatives and if appropriate make improvements on past approaches. The process can begin again, highlighting the cyclical nature of the PIC©

The Performance Improvement Cycle© thus provides:

- A structured methodology that can be applied to both hard and soft skills training interventions.
- An evidence based approach to L&D which will be very well received by executives.
- An approach that supports behavioural change and enables new skills to be embedded into the organisation.
- Return on investment results setting out the outputs from the training

Moving away from existing practises will require a change in thinking to ensure all learning and development leads to improved bottom line performance. The Performance Improvement Cycle© will enable organisations to facilitate the necessary change and in doing so will ensure an improved return on investment and thus increased competitiveness.

CASE STUDIES

Each of the case studies shows how the Performance Improvement Cycle© has supported and shaped the learning initiative. We have grouped elements of the cycle to make it easy to follow the sequence, although each case study is individual and the format is not always identical.

- Summary
- Background
- Evaluation and Benchmark
- Targets
- Intervention and Transfer
- Measurement and Evaluation
- Return on Investment
- Conclusions and learning

Please note that the case studies used in this book are anonymous. Should the reader wish to obtain further information on a case study, contact us directly at www.gpsvision.co.uk or 02476 223110.

There is a summary of the case study key findings in Chapter 12.

CHAPTER 4

DEVELOPING THE LEADERSHIP TEAM

Organisation A conducted an organisation wide management development programme and delivered significant Return on Investment savings by focusing improvements in four main areas, communication with staff, developing staff, managing conflict and tackling poor performance.

Background

In June 2006, Organisation A carried out a review of its management development needs across the organisation. This was to provide a starting point for a management development programme to support strategic aims for the next ten years. This involved in-depth interviews with directors, managers and staff and resulted in the following findings based on majority views:

- A leadership programme will improve the company's performance
- A formal qualification is a good idea
- 75% of managers have not previously been on a leadership programme
- A practical programme, underpinned by theory, is more appropriate than a purely academic programme
- A suitable programme would be tailored to the housing sector
- The programme should be delivered away from the workplace and externally delivered
- Assessment should include a work based project

We were asked to work with them, due to our considerable experience of working in the housing sector. Using the Performance Improvement Cycle© to support the learning process, we formulated a plan for the development programme. (Figure 4)

Figure 4 Performance Improvement Cycle© Process for Organisation A

PIC© Stages	Outputs
Evaluation	An audit of the current situation through interviews with senior managers
Benchmarking	A self evaluation of management skills by all identified participants in both Senior and Middle management group.
Targets	Improving management skills (see below) Improving organisational targets
Intervention	CMI Accredited Programmes
Transfer	Action Learning, Line Manager Support, Study Support.
Measure	Outcomes against targets
Evaluation	Review and calculate return on investment.

Evaluation and Benchmarking

The initial evaluation phase, as described above, identified the following areas as key management skills areas that needed addressing:

- Communication skills
- Developing staff
- Managing conflict
- Poor performance

To further investigate this, benchmarking was established by using a self evaluation skills based questionnaire with programme participants, prior to the start.

Participants were required to discuss their pre-programme questionnaire results with their line managers in a one-to-one review session. The focus was to discuss the findings and identify how the programme could be used to improve the results. Motivation to learn and ability to apply the learning were also assessed at this point, and produced very positive feedback. These replies led us to design an induction session for line managers, to ensure strategies were in place to support participants and eliminate any barriers to learning.

As a result, we agreed the appropriate intervention to be a Level 4 Introductory Diploma in Management (CMI qualification) for 20 middle managers. Where the benchmarking exercise had highlighted needs outside the formal programme, additional learning material was included, such as negotiation and managing conflict.

The next stage in the Performance Improvement Cycle© was to set organisational targets to close the gaps between the Key Performance Indicators' current results and the desired results.

Targets

Organisational targets were:

- Reduce turnover by 2%
- Reduce short term absence by 1%
- Achieve Investors In People status by August 2007
- Achieve 90% customer satisfaction with repairs
- Achieve 90% customer satisfaction with lettings service
- Achieve 99% of repairs appointments kept
- Reduce arrears by 1.5%

Intervention and Transfer

Five workshops, including action learning sessions were delivered in house by GPSVision over a three month period along with two half-day study support sessions.

Participants were expected to complete and submit an assignment to achieve the CMI qualification, and to complete a project that delivered performance improvements to their department and the organisation as a whole.

A communications plan was developed to inform staff across the business and this transparency increased not only dialogue about the programme, but also raised expectations. The programme cost was £1,000 per participant of which 50% was raised through a national development initiative to improve management and leadership skills, managed by Business Link.

Measurement and Evaluation

Reaction

Participants responded well to the workshops and more importantly were positive about the relevance and opportunity to apply the learning. Participants rated all aspects of the five workshops at an average score of 4.46 out of 5 over the study period.

- *A better understanding of other teams and the pressures they face to meet deadlines*
- *Belbin was interesting, made me more self aware*
- *The tutor has a very positive, enjoyable way of teaching, which keeps you involved & interested*
- *Another enjoyable day, good group participation*
- *Thank you!*
- *Discussion within group was eye opening and supportive*
- *Very enjoyable and informative*

Participants CMI Programme Organisation A

Learning

The organisation achieved a 100% pass rate and all managers were presented with their CMI certificates at an award ceremony to acknowledge their efforts and reinforce the need to continue with their behavioural change and good practice.

Behavioural change

The graph at Figure 5 shows the significant movement in scores in the pre- and post- self evaluation questionnaire results.

Figure 5 Before and after self evaluation management skills (Organisation A)

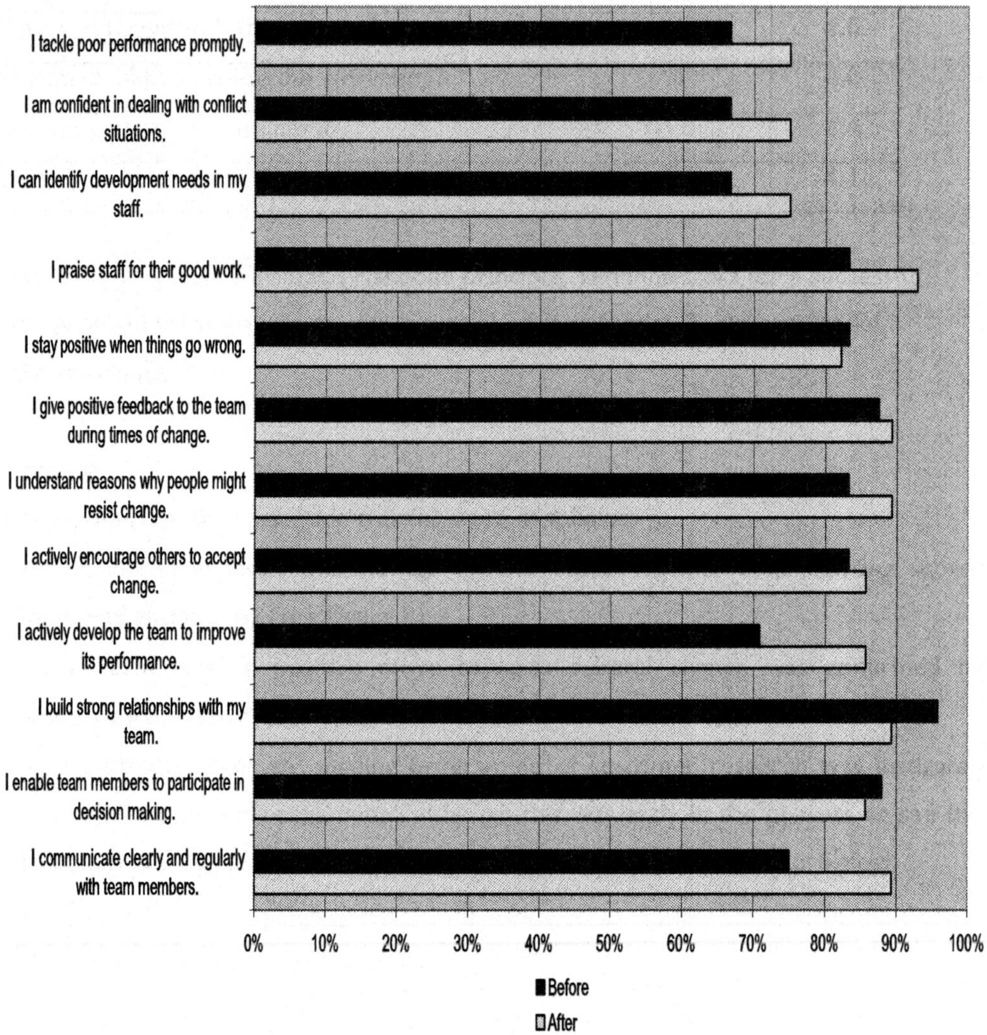

The five lower starting scores showed significant improvement and action learning sessions were provided to continue this progress. We were delighted that all areas now received a rating of 75% or more. Although some scores had gone down slightly, this is not an uncommon factor when starting scores are high.

Organisational impact

To date Organisation A has generated considerable savings by following the Performance Improvement Cycle© as summarised below in Figure 6

Figure 6 Organisation A performance targets and outcomes

Target	Outcomes
Reduce staff turnover by 2%	Achieved
Reduce short term absence by 1%	Partly achieved (0.5%)
Achieve IIP status in August 2007	Achieved with very positive results
Achieve 90% customer satisfaction with repairs	Outperformed + (93%)
Achieve 90% customer satisfaction with lettings service	Achieved
Achieve 99% of repairs appointments kept	Partly achieved (98.5%)
Reduce arrears by 1.5%	Outperformed + (1.8%)

Return on Investment

The performance against the organisation targets has saved over £85,000 which equates to a 750% Return on Investment against a £10,000 investment in the programme. This figure is achieved from only three of the above targets; staff turnover, short term absence and improved arrears collection. The other targets have also delivered significant intangible benefits to customers.

In addition to these quantifiable benefits, positive behavioural change has also been experienced, evaluated through a self reporting impact review and discussion with senior managers. Participants are more confident and are more inclined to request help and guidance around operational issues, leading to a more pro-active and successful approach to problem solving. Inter departmental relationships have also improved and there is more trust and sharing around operational challenges.

Overall we are delighted with these results. Managers have responded very well to the programme; show increased levels of skill and competence and we have raised the academic levels across the organisation.

Head of Human Resources Organisation A

Shown as an ROI figure equates to:

$$\frac{\text{Benefit from training} - \text{cost of training} \times 100}{\text{Cost of training}} = \text{ROI\%}$$

$$\frac{£85000 - £10000 \times 100}{£10000} = 750\%$$

In conclusion

Setting clear targets is vital to being able to measure the outcomes at the end of a programme. If organisations' performance indicators are transparent and clear to everyone it is far more likely that return on investment can be identified.

Some of the questions that need to be asked are:

- What is the business objective?
- What are the issues we need to address?
- What are the targets we need to set for individuals, teams, customers and the business?
- What is the appropriate learning intervention?
- What should the learning transfer strategy include?
- What timescales should be set around the process and evaluation plan?

CHAPTER 5

MANAGING ORGANISATIONAL CHANGE

Organisation B was tasked with integrating a Direct Labour Organisation into their established business. This proved a challenge in managing the change in both culture and practice, to achieve a positive outcome for all parties.

Background

The decision by a housing organisation to bring repair and maintenance services in-house involved integrating 170 employees as part of a TUPE transfer. This included 145 craft workers (plumbers, electricians, painters and carpenters, etc).

An appraisal of the business identified the need to reduce expenditure by at least £1m for the business to be cost effective. To achieve this, the organisation needed to reduce costs, increase productivity, reduce sickness absence and increase business outputs. The business solution was complex and included business process re-engineering, restructuring the organisation and changing many unproductive working practices. During the implementation of these changes, the organisation also needed to maintain an effective service to customers which meant maintaining morale during a time of change.

This case study concentrates on one aspect of the overall business solution, which was the introduction of twelve team leader posts as part of the restructuring proposals. Each of the team leaders had responsibility for the performance and productivity of around 12 craft workers.

Evaluation and Benchmark

Two options were identified that would deliver the improved leadership approach:

- Recruit new team leaders with the required management skills and experience.
- Equip existing staff to take on the team leader's role, by providing the necessary management and leadership skills.

Organisation B decided that the second option, if successful, would provide a better return on investment. In discussion with us, they opted for a formal leadership development programme, using the Performance Improvement Cycle© to plan, deliver and track results.

> *Clearly this presented a cost effective business solution with a great ROI*
>
> Organisational Development Director Organisation B

It is not just about numbers and calculations; often there are deeper returns in addition to financial ones. The return on investment within the wider business context was also evaluated looking at outputs that were not converted to a cash ROI. For example, the opportunity that the initiative gave to achieve Investors in People (IiP) in the department is another justification for the expenditure on learning.

It is also important to achieve a positive return on investment for the learners as well as for the business. The twelve employees that undertook leadership development were committed for a number of reasons, the most obvious being job security. They could see it made business sense for them to succeed. They were also able to submit assessed work to gain a BTEC Level 4 management qualification. Most of this group had no previous management qualifications so this was seen as a valuable opportunity for the individuals as well as the organisation.

The next step was to conduct a benchmarking exercise. We needed to drill down and identify the issues that would need to be addressed at the intervention phase.

Previously in the pre-transfer organisation, the workforce had failed Investors in People accreditation and had a culture that disempowered employees. The supervisors had been promoted internally and had risen from "the tools". The IiP assessment showed that many did not see their role as managing the workforce. They had certainly never had any leadership or management development in the past, and they were very unclear about the expectations on them as team leaders.

To complete the benchmarking process all team leaders completed an APTER[xvii]™ motivational style diagnostic and a GPSVision skills assessment. They had a 1-1 coaching review with a learning consultant, enabling each to set some personal learning objectives. These could then be measured following the learning intervention, to establish personal improvement.

Targets

The next stage in the Performance Improvement Cycle© was to establish the outcomes sought and these were identified under four headings. (Figure 7)

Figure 7 Targets for improvement Organisation B

Individual	Team	Organisation	Customer
Communicate the vision	Inclusive culture	Effective structure	Quality job first time
Tackle poor performance	Praise culture	Feedback systems	All appointments kept
Set smart objectives	Equitable allocation of jobs to trades-people	Maintain business turnover (£)	Clean working
Motivating and praising the workforce	Improved morale	Reduced absence levels	Polite and respectful
Achieve team leader status		Achieve Investors in People	

- At the team level, targets were set that were linked to the transformation of the organisational culture.
- At the customer level there were also clear targets set from the outcome of customer satisfaction surveys that again could be measured after the learning had been implemented.

The benchmarking exercises identified a range of issues against which targets were set. At this stage, we developed the specific learning programme with the Organisational Development Team.

This is where I have made the mistake in the past, by diving straight into throwing some training at the problem and then wondering why nothing seems to change, or why it's hard to evaluate or show a return on investment!
We can easily fall into the trap that putting people through some training is the objective rather than the training is the intervention to achieve business objectives. I have certainly been asked in the past to put managers through a leadership programme; I now ask what are the objectives and what do you want to achieve?

Organisational Development Director Organisation B

Intervention and Transfer

The chosen intervention was a BTEC Level 4 Professional Award accredited by Edexel, in Leadership and Performance Management. We decided to deliver this in half day workshops, acknowledging that the programme participants were unfamiliar with this type of learning environment.

We discussed with the group of learners how best to help them to apply their learning in the workplace. Many requested line manager support, so we met with their managers to brief them about the programme and their role within it.

Anecdotally, one participant told us that he felt he didn't need to attend as he had been on previous management development training. Later, he observed that his previous experience had not included any expectation of demonstrating change to his practice. This was the first time, he observed, that he was expected to change as a result of attending a development programme.

> *A learning transfer strategy is a critical aspect of the learning process. If it is not in place then the investment is not likely to be fully realised.*
>
> Patrick Taggart GPSVision

Measurement and Evaluation

Reaction The final part of the Performance Improvement Cycle© is to measure the success of the training. The table below provides a précis of the "happy sheet" scores (maximum 5).

How valuable was the workshop for your current role?	**4.0**
Were you happy with the content?	**4.0**
How much did you enjoy the workshop?	**4.0**
How did you rate the trainers?	**4.4**
Will you be able to use the learning in your own workplace?	**4.1**

Positive learning points included Fishbone principle, Ten Indicators for a successful team, problem solving exercise with 'post its' , Adairs Model, Tuckmans Model, Problem solving.

Learning

Key outputs from the leadership training were as follows:

- At an individual level, the average learner scores against their starting scores improved significantly (see Figure 8).
- At a Team level, a positive move towards cultural change was confirmed by feedback from trade unions and craft workers.
- At a customer level, an ongoing programme of customer research was instigated and demonstrated improvements, although this was early in the process to see the full knock-on effects of improved leadership, and remains a work in progress.

Behavioural change

Figure 8 Before and after scores for Organisation B

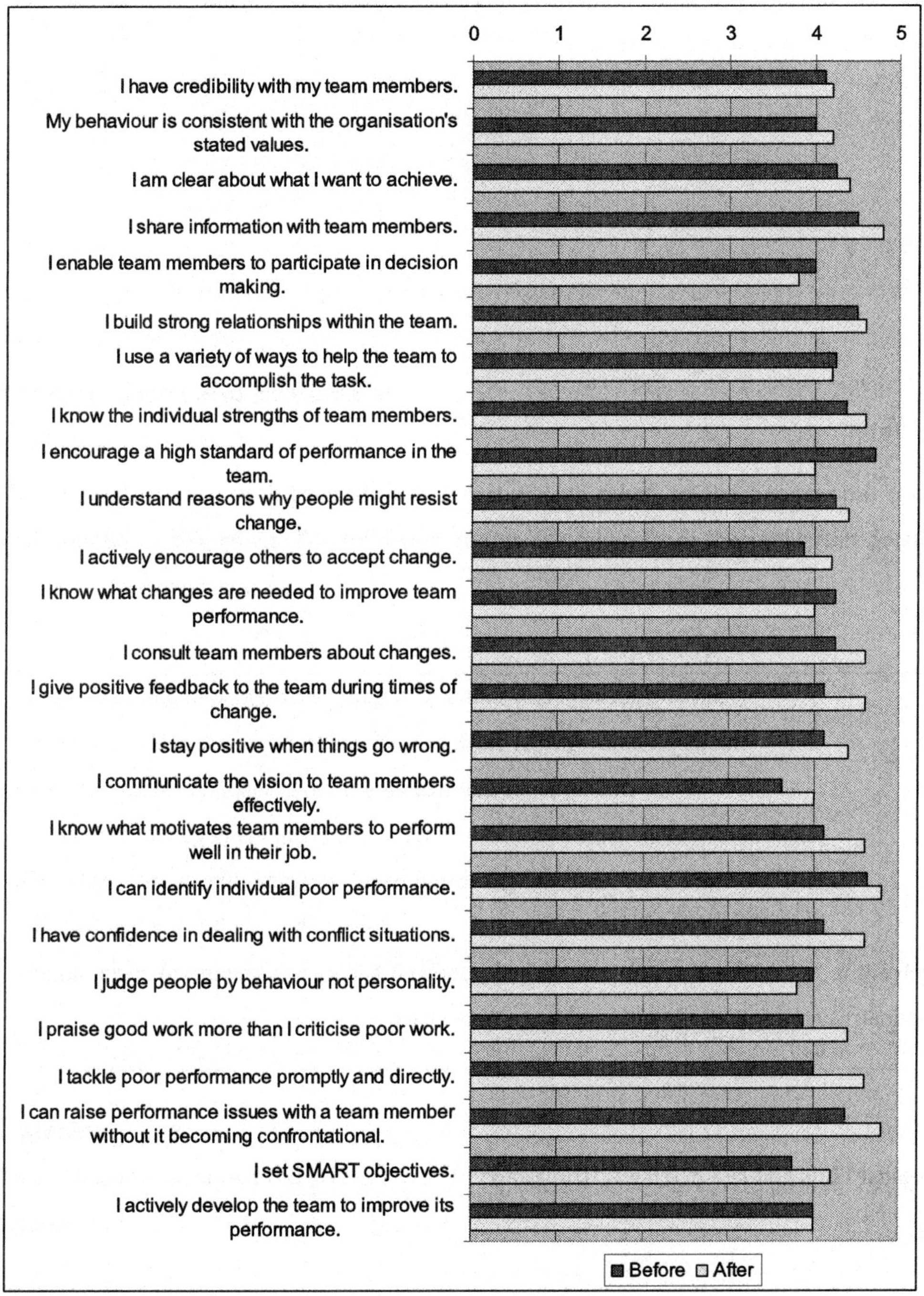

Organisational impact

At an organisational level, Investors in People was achieved in 2007. The restructuring proved successful and the business maintained its turnover levels. The savings from reduction in absence levels, reduced recruitment costs and avoidance of redundancy costs were all achieved.

Return on Investment

The financial Return on Investment results were as follows:

Reduction in redundancy costs	£80,000
Saving of recruitment costs	£7,500
Reduction in sickness absence by 2%.	£75,000

Shown as an ROI figure equates to:

$$\frac{\textbf{Benefit from training – cost of training x 100}}{\textbf{Cost of training}} = \textbf{ROI\%}$$

$$\frac{\textbf{£162500 - £15000 x 100}}{\textbf{£15000}} = \textbf{983\%}$$

In conclusion

It is important to take into account the learners' preferences for learning and their past learning experiences. It is also important to check the learners' expectations as this will increase engagement levels and the application of new skills.

In this example, the submission of assignments was variable with only 50% of participants gaining the qualification. Part of the problem here was the level of change that was going on at the time. The programme was intended to facilitate that change, but it is clear that the level of commitment required to complete the assignment was a step too far for some.

In future projects of this kind we would build in more assessment support during the workshops and encourage line managers to become more involved in this area.

CHAPTER 6

DEVELOPING TALENT

GPSVision supported Organisation C in implementing a Leading Change Programme which led to savings in excess of £44,000. This initiative addressed the need for more efficient working, developing talent and the creation of a succession planning culture.

Background

In the spring of 2004, the Senior Management Team within Organisation C identified the need to address the management skills shortages within their Division. Most of the senior team felt under pressure from additional work generated by new initiatives, such as business planning and target tracking, introduced into the NHS to tackle performance issues. As a result, they believed that by increasing the management capacity within the Division, this would lead to better results, maintain a high quality of clinical work and also increase the capacity to innovate and change services for the better. Senior managers nominated staff with strong leadership potential and following a selection process, twenty three people were selected as participants for the development programme.

Evaluation and Benchmarking

This large Division of the Trust consisted of a multiplicity of professional groups, and middle managers had little knowledge of each other either personally or professionally. There was no culture of succession planning throughout the Division; however senior managers believed that this was not due to a lack of potential but due to a lack of exposure to responsibility and decision making at the required level.

Three organisational outcomes from the programme were identified:

- Improved Leadership and Management skills
- Improve the succession planning options within the Division
- Better communication and networking between senior and middle managers

The senior team engaged GPSVision to deliver a BTEC level 4 Leadership programme which was accredited and awarded by Edexel, supported by the PIC© methodology (see Chapter 2).

The team had strong views on the format and outcomes of the programme and worked closely with GPSVision to design and develop a suitable programme using the Performance Improvement Cycle© planning framework as a road map. A number of participant objectives were identified for this initiative which were:

- Using a work based project as a vehicle for personal and organisational improvement linked to patient care
- Ensuring that personal performance improvement could be demonstrated and measured
- Ensure participants received a relevant formal qualification

A 180° skills audit was carried out by the line manager and participant at the beginning and end of the programme. This enabled assessment of the level of improvement by individual and group.

Targets

Targets were set for the senior managers and the participants. See Figures 9 and 10 below.

Figure 9 Target Learning Outcomes: Senior Management Organisation C

Senior and Line Manager Targets
Coach their team through the development process
Conduct thorough pre and post development reviews
Set practical opportunities to help staff apply new skills and practices
Conduct performance reviews focusing on skills gaps and identify opportunities that can be used to bridge these
Carry out effective action learning sets to facilitate the application of new skills to the workplace
Confidently delegate tasks to team members
Operate more strategically via delegating more hands on tasks to a more competent team

Figure 10 Target Learning Outcomes for Delegates Organisation C

Delegates Targets
Explain five differences between leadership and management and assess how these differences relate to the manager's own role
Explain three different leadership models in the context of the manager's own workplace
Undertake an initial evaluation of current personal emotional intelligence and devise a plan to develop EQ including proposals for action planning, monitoring and evaluation
Describe a change process that you have been involved in and evaluate how successful that change process has been. Investigate actions for improvement, or reasons for success
Devise a team development plan which will assist you in achieving a flexible and responsive team which handles change successfully
Devise a project plan for a current issue within the workplace, to include a communication and consultation plan, and the steps that you will take to monitor and evaluate the project
Critically analyse and compare different performance review schemes including company specific procedures
Set smart targets for an identified project within the workplace
Undertake an appraisal or performance review and give a reflective commentary on it
Produce a plan for an individual case study which investigates poor performance and describes steps for improvement, including review mechanisms

Intervention and Transfer

The Senior Team attended a two day workshop to plan the programme and determine the level of support required to ensure the participants could apply their new knowledge and skills back into the workplace. Workshops were organised on a timetabled basis with two flexible work streams organised so that delegates could choose which date was most convenient. This enhanced the communication and team spirit so they became one team rather than two cohorts. The key elements of the programme were as follows:

The programme began with a lunchtime induction session with presentations of rationale and content by the Senior Management Team and GPSVision. The learners were introduced to the idea of keeping developmental portfolios which were to act as evidence towards their qualification. This was to be a record showing how the learning had been embedded in their working practice.

Key to the programme was the concept of delivering a work based project. This project was enhanced because of the increased access to colleagues, trainers and programme knowledge. All projects delivered system and patient improvements across the Trust. Presentations were given to the Core Management team to demonstrate outcomes from the project, benefits to the Division, the Trust and patients. This also improved the participants' confidence and skill when presenting in a professional and pressurised environment.

Each participant was offered a named mentor within the Senior Management Team. The programme also included time for participants to discuss each module with their line manager before and after each study day. Work shadowing opportunities with the Executive Team of the Trust and the Senior Management Team of the Division were offered to all participants.

Action learning sets were included throughout the programme, which helped to apply the new knowledge and skills to current operational issues.

Measurement and Evaluation

Reaction

The delegates were very pleased with the approach taken to the programme and have commented to this effect. The following quotes are taken from the evaluation documents and at review meetings:

> *A well organised and interactive programme that was invaluable to me*
>
> *It was very relevant and the afternoon energisers reinvigorated my brain*
>
> *I now feel more confident about the assessment requirements*
>
> *The Project Management guide was useful*
>
> *Role plays were useful - they can be embarrassing but these were short and fruitful*
>
> *The environment is lively and relaxed*
>
> *I do not enjoy presenting and getting feedback, but this time it was the best part of the day*
>
> Participants Leading Change Programme Organisation C

Learning

19 participants obtained the BTEC Level 4 Professional Award in Leading and Managing Change.

Behavioural change

Figure 11 180° pre and post evaluations Organisation C

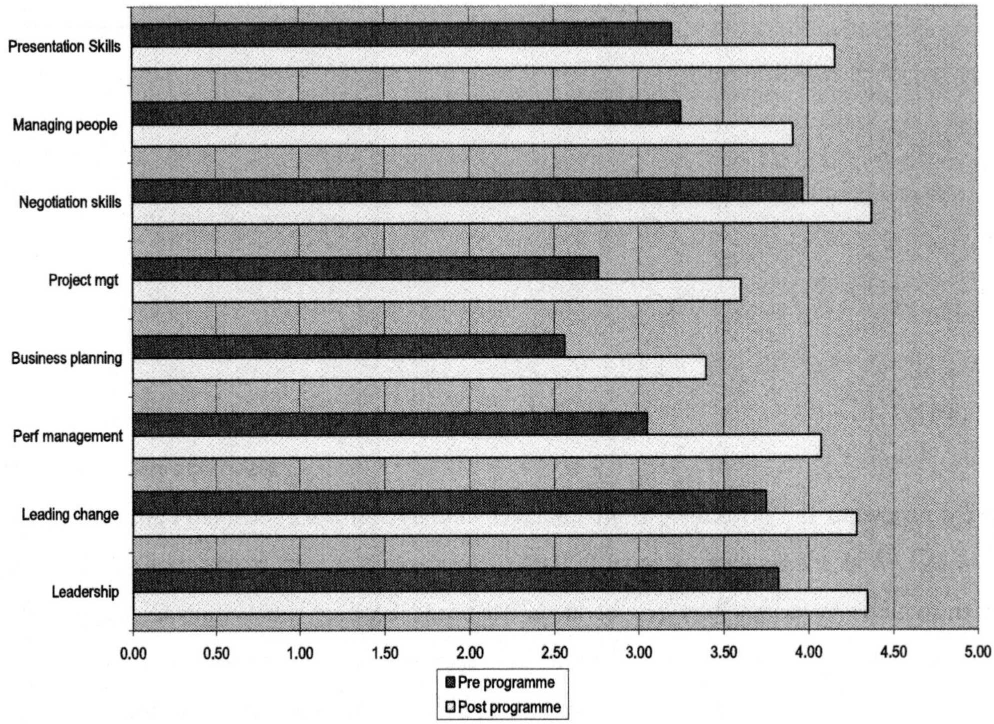

Organisational impact

The programme also delivered the following intangible benefits to the organisation:

- Increased decision making input from staff
- Improved managerial skills of the middle tier managers
- Teams responding more quickly to change and developing implementation plans
- A reduction in conflict situations that create tension within teams
- An increase in staff motivation via more effective performance reviews
- Improved inter-departmental working developed over the course of the programme
- Improved budgetary control and liaison with the finance team
- Better influencing skills through enhanced presentation skills
- Tighter project management resulting in improved deadline achievement and control
- Departmental improvements resulting from the completion of the work based projects

Return on Investment

An initial evaluation showed that two of the projects alone realised savings to the Trust of £44,000 against the cost of the programme at £25,000, resulting in a net return of £19,000. Further projects having longer term effects were expected to deliver further savings.

Showing these savings as an ROI result is:

$$\frac{\text{Benefit from training} - \text{cost of training}}{\text{Cost of training}} \times 100 = \text{ROI\%}$$

$$\frac{£44000 - £25000}{£25000} \times 100 = 76\%$$

In conclusion

We recognised the importance of real projects in helping to establish the return on investment from a training programme. Participants had to plan, manage and report on a chosen project, and were asked to present this to an audience which included the Senior Management Team of the Division.

All of the projects delivered significant improvements to service as well as cost savings and while some were very simple to evaluate in cash terms, others could be measured in terms of quality rather than quantity. It is important to be able to identify intangible as well as tangible outputs.

Another important factor was the commitment of Senior Management within this Division to the programme. They had identified people who they believed could be stretched and would add significant value to the Division. They enhanced the value of the learning by staying close to the programme and by offering a lot of support to participants. Our experience has taught us that when 'programme champions' disengage or lose interest the impact results are greatly reduced.

CHAPTER 7

FACING COMPETITION

Organisation D delivered a ROI of 545% and improved its competitiveness. This was achieved through a management development programme that improved productivity and focused on the organisation's core values.

Background

This case study looks at how a charitable organisation generated a large Return on Investment by following the Performance Improvement Cycle©. The organisation was established with the aim of reducing alcohol and drug related harm and promoting informed choices about the use of alcohol and other addictive substances and behaviours. Typical work areas include individual alcohol and drug counselling, cognitive behavioural therapy, group work and family work.

Evaluation and Benchmarking

A new Chief Executive had been appointed, and she was keen to implement performance improvement initiatives across the whole organisation. The marketplace was becoming more competitive and in order to face this challenge, managers needed to be more productive and be able to get more from their teams, whilst maintaining core values:

- A belief in people's ability to change and their right to be empowered to do so
- The valuing of difference and diversity
- Recognition of the significance of social factors and particularly social disadvantage in influencing behaviour and changes

The charity acknowledged a need to up-skill their leaders and managers across the organisation and approached us to work with them to achieve this objective. The overall aim of the leadership development programme was to develop the managers into a highly effective and confident group, who could lead and motivate their teams. In addition the following specific targets were set:

Targets

Figure 12 Targets for improvement Organisation D

	Current situation	Target
Absence	8%	6%
Staff turnover	12%	10%
Promotions from within the group	0	3
Information requests	Slow response rate	100% within 5 working days

All of these targets were to be achieved within 12 months of the programme completion. The chosen programme was not accredited, therefore it was important to be able to track learning and behavioural change through the setting of personal goals and targets for individual participants.

In order to benchmark the individual skills sets, a 180° questionnaire was used prior to the start of the programme to establish the starting point of the individuals concerned. This can be seen below at figure 14 and shows the pre programme and post programme results. The pre programme results were used to help GPSVision develop relevant content for the workshops.

Intervention and Transfer

GPSVision ran four workshops with the theme of 'Effective People Management' covering a wide range of areas including recruitment and selection, induction, competence frameworks, appraisal and performance reviews, processes for managing discipline and grievances, staff development and developing outstanding team performance. These workshops were scheduled over a period of four months, to enable embedding and goal setting to take place between the formal learning sessions.

The organisation considered accrediting the learning, but decided against it due to cost pressures.

Measurement and Evaluation

The impact of the programme was measured by using pre and post programme questionnaires, verbal feedback and face to face meetings. Post programme data was sought at three and six month's stages after the last formal session. Data was tracked and collected against five key areas.

Reaction

A summary of the post workshop feedback was very positive with all scores averaging 4+ out of 5. In particular the score for question 5 is both very important and very positive.

Figure 13 Reaction level feedback: Leadership Programme for Organisation D

How valuable was the workshop to your current role?	4.3
Were you happy with the content?	4.2
How much did you enjoy the workshops?	4.2
How did you rate the trainers?	4.5
Will you be able to use the learning in your own workplace?	4.4

Learning

The second level of measurement was the extent of learning achieved. To assess this, managers were asked to provide quantitative feedback on the range of questions where the score of 100% means fully effective and 0% not able to demonstrate effectiveness (Figure 14).

Figure 14 Evidence of learning through 180° questionnaire analysis Organisation D

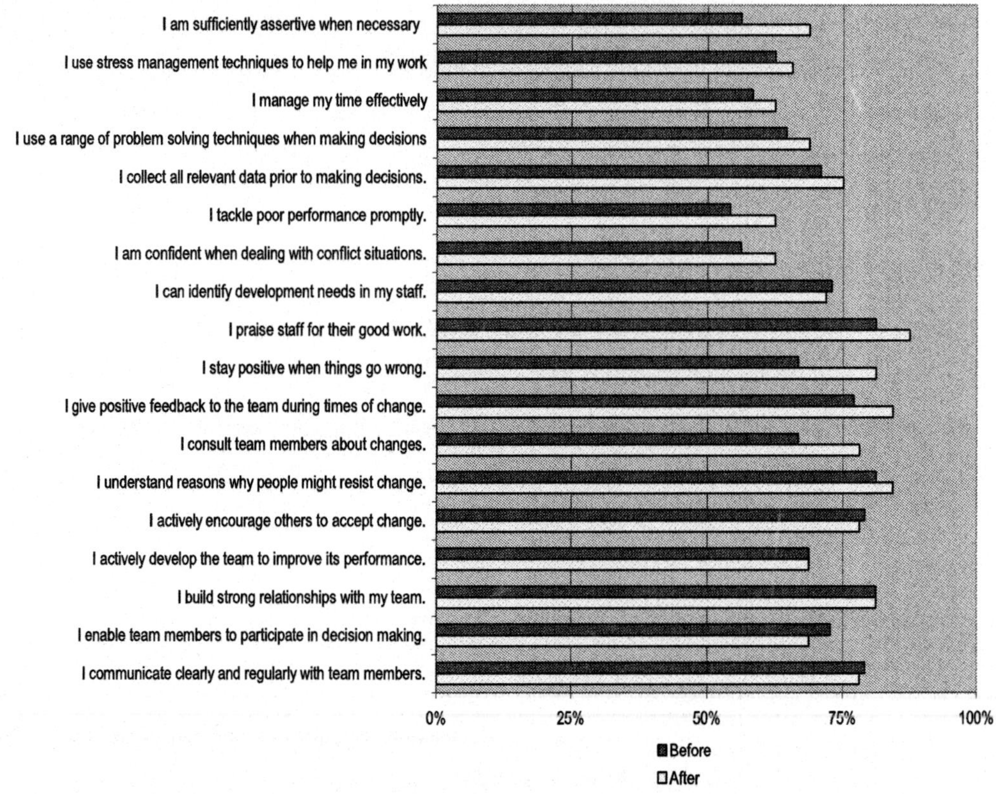

Significant improvements are shown against:

I consult team members about changes I give positive feedback to the team during times of change I stay positive when things go wrong I praise staff for good work	I am confident when dealing with conflict situations I tackle poor performance promptly I am sufficiently assertive when necessary

Behavioural change

Participants were asked to provide feedback on how they had changed and/or used their learning to improve their performance. We have set out a sample of their feedback below:

I now identify problems with staff, such as lateness and talk to staff immediately in order to resolve the issue. I am doing this as often as I can, and have a late book in place and address issues at staff meetings as well as one to one.
I now think more creatively and action more creative thinking in my work plans and ideas. I am determined to look at things from all angles, force myself to step back, reflect, and bought a plant, picture and cards for my office for inspiration – stayed de-cluttered.
I have implemented new triage and comprehensive client assessment forms. We have implemented a simple and organised system to help ensure that the new forms are being used.
I feel I am more confident and assertive in dealing with staff competency and performance issues. I have dealt with recent performance and competence issues well.
I am more objective and dispassionate in my supervision and have found ways to keep emotions in the background. I continue to discuss and progress this with my manager
I am working on improving my IT skills although this has been slow.

Organisational impact

The organisational impact looks at how the programme has impacted individuals/their team, the organisation and customers. Clearly there has been some real progress and the managers should be proud of their efforts. Specific organisational impacts include:

- Staff are clearer about their roles and responsibilities and work more effectively
- The standardisation of forms and relocation of data has made us more efficient
- Some potentially negligent practice has been avoided and supervisees are more organised

> *We believe the programme has helped our managers to tackle their roles in a more confident and analytical manner, which achieves our overall aim at the outset of the programme.*
>
> Chief Executive, Organisation D

Return on Investment

By applying the Performance Improvement Cycle©, the organisation has delivered a 545% return on investment to date and savings of £46,000 from an investment of £7,125 in the programme. Savings were realised based on absence and staff turnover reductions and recruitment cost savings as one manager has been promoted, which saved recruiting externally. Return on investment (Figure 15) was calculated as follows:

Figure 15 Return on Investment for Organisation D

Target	Result	Cash return
Reduce absence from 8% to 6% within 12 months	Reduced to 7%	£10,000
Reduce staff turnover from 12% to 10% within 12 months	Reduced to 7%	£30,000
3 of the group to achieve promotion within 12 months	1 promoted	£6,000
Managers to respond within 5 days to all requests for information	Work in progress	nil

The above figures can be shown as a percentage ROI figure by using the accepted formula:

$$\frac{\text{Benefit from training} - \text{cost of training} \times 100}{\text{Cost of training}} = \text{ROI\%}$$

$$\frac{£46000 - £7125 \times 100}{£7125} = 545\%$$

An evaluation meeting with the Chief Executive six months after the final workshop provided the following comments:

Managers are more interested in the bigger picture and how our current services affect future funding opportunities. We have noticed improved inter departmental working at our Heads of Division team meetings. It is very clear that our managers will require additional support to apply the learning and make the necessary behavioural changes to improve their output and our business further

We are pleased with the incremental improvements mentioned to date and are pleased that it has been possible to convert some of the changes to a cash return on investment. This was not our key driver but the Performance Improvement Cycle© has made this possible. The savings have allowed us to provide our customers with some very useful additional services

Chief Executive, Organisation D

In conclusion

The Third Sector, previously known as Voluntary Sector, is made up of charitable and not-for-profit organisations. Over the last twenty years this sector has become increasingly businesslike, and has taken on responsibility for much service provision in areas such as social care, previously carried out by the public sector.

The result of this has been a growth in organisations competing for funding, needing to demonstrate excellence in practice and business skills. To meet this challenge, it is vital that not only professional and technical, but leadership and management skills are in place. In this case it was a vision of the chief executive who recognised the need to improve leadership and management skills across the organisation.

The decision was made not to accredit the programme and in retrospect we believe that this was a mistake. Generally we find accredited programmes provide a useful stage in the validation of learning and by forcing the participant to reflect, this increases their content retention levels. This increased level of retention gives participants more chance of applying their new learning which ultimately leads to increased behavioural change and return on investment.

CHAPTER 8

SUPPORTING CULTURAL CHANGE

Organisation E used a leadership development programme to support its cultural change strategy, generating a 67% Return on Investment. Organisation E had recently been transferred from local authority control, following a successful tenant vote. Prior opportunities for management development had been limited and this was seen as an opportunity to embed culture change as well as to increase the skills base of the organisation.

Background

Organisation E is a newly created Housing Association managing a portfolio of almost 4,000 properties plus land and garages. Having just made the transition to independent status, the Senior Team wanted to ensure that managers had the leadership skills needed to operate effectively in the new environment. The twin aims of the leadership programme were to develop:

- a highly effective and confident wider management team, able to lead and motivate staff in a time of major change
- a culture reflecting the new agenda that focused on performance improvement

Evaluation and Benchmarking

Organisation E approached GPSVision to deliver the programme which was seen as central to the transition strategy. Due to the new nature of the business venture, it was difficult to gather comparative data at the start of the programme; therefore we focused on individual development and implementation of personal objectives to measure the outcome of the programme. The benchmarking exercise involved a 360° skills evaluation for each participant, which would be reviewed at the end of the programme.

Targets

The main aims of the leadership programme were to up skill and develop the confidence levels of a group of managers who had been neglected in their roles with the council. Three targets were set:

- Build a highly effective and confident wider management team, able to lead and motivate staff in a time of major change
- Build a culture reflecting the new agenda that focuses on performance improvement
- Increase the academic base of the managers and reward them for their application and hard work

Intervention and Transfer

The intervention chosen was a formal qualification, and in consultation with the Senior Team we chose a Level 4 Introductory Diploma in Management accredited by the Chartered Management Institute. This is a generic programme offering an introduction to a broad range of management knowledge and skills.

The five workshops offered a basic introduction to a range of management and leadership models and techniques.

- Developing your management style
- Managing projects and working with others
- Planning and managing resources
- Managing information and communicating
- Focusing on customers and promoting the business

The Diploma is assessed through submitted coursework and we gave two study support surgeries and offered significant formative feedback. This level of support helped the participants overcome their fears about the written work and the group study sessions encouraged commitment and completion rates.

Measurement and Evaluation

Reaction

Figure 16 Reaction Level feedback Organisation E

Workshop	1	2	3	4	5
How valuable was the workshop for your current role?	4.1	4.3	3.9	3.9	4
Were you happy with the content?	4.1	4.4	3.9	4	4.1
How much did you enjoy the workshop?	4.2	4.4	3.6	3.9	4.1
How did you rate the trainers?	4.4	4.6	4.4	4.6	4.4
Will you be able to use the learning in your own workplace?	3.8	4.2	3.8	3.8	4

Overall participants were satisfied with the sessions with most scores exceeding 4 on a scale of 1 = poor and 5 = excellent. However we did need to encourage dialogue between the participants and their line managers to address the scope for using the learning in their jobs. Additionally session 3 was reviewed and for future groups was made more practical.

Learning

One key indicator for assessing learning was the successful completion of coursework to achieve the Introductory Diploma in Management and 12 out of the 15 learners achieved this.

In addition we asked participants to provide feedback on their key learning points and the table below provides a sample of the results:

Figure 17 Reported positive learning outcomes Organisation E

The delegation, motivation and tackling poor performance workshops were particularly helpful to me

Team working, project management and effective delegation stood out for me

Effective recruitment and selection

The benefits of delegating to improve team development and the difference between delegating and dumping were helpful sessions

Participants CMI Introductory Diploma Organisation E

Behavioural change

Figure 18 360° Evaluation scores before and after the programme Organisation E

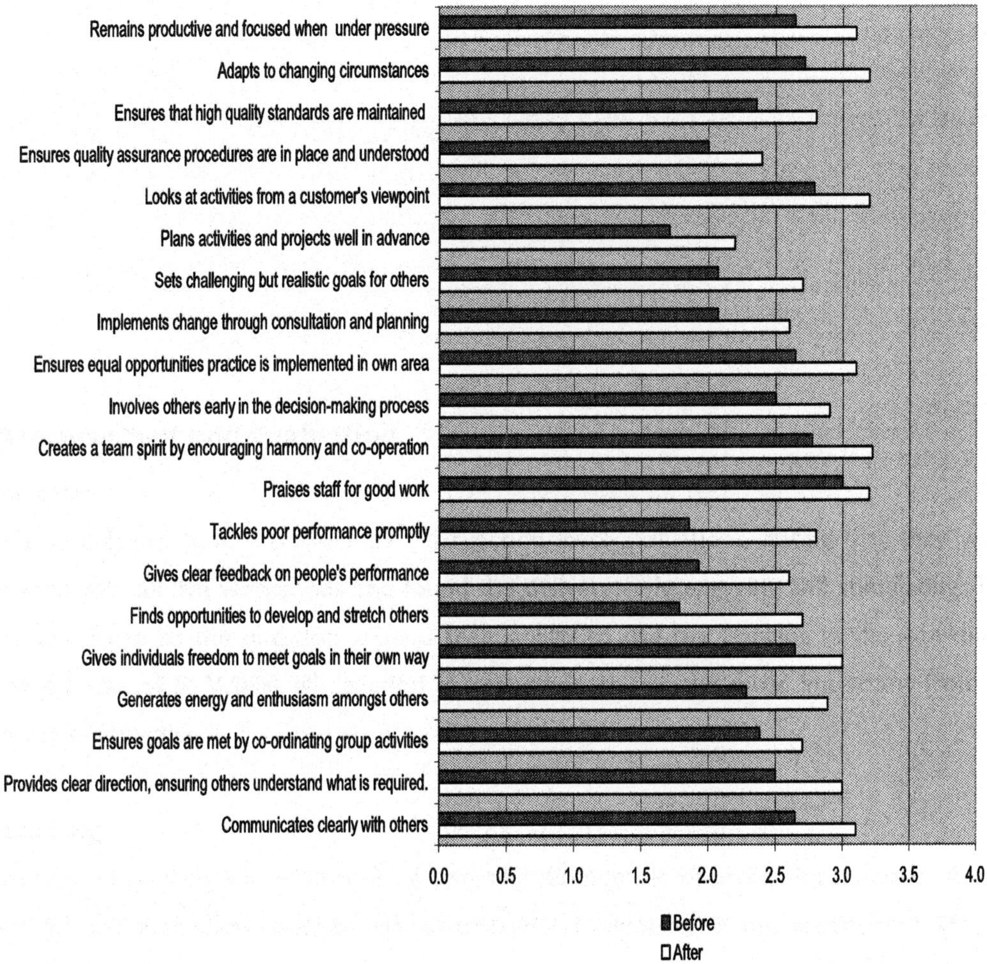

4	3	2	1
excellent	good	satisfactory	needs improvement

The post programme review of skills took place approximately six months after the completion of the programme, allowing time for managers to embed their learning in practice. Comparison of the pre-programme and post-programme 360° questionnaires showed improvement in all areas.

The five highest improvements were:

- Setting challenging goals
- Tackling poor performance promptly
- Providing clear feedback on performance
- Finding opportunities to develop and stretch others
- Generating energy and enthusiasm amongst others

These factors were exactly the types of improvements required to achieve the organisational goal of developing a performance improvement culture.

Figure 19 below also shows the impact of the new learning measured by collecting data from the participant, their line manager, staff and colleagues. Most participant scores show an upward trend although in some cases we were unable to collect pre and post data for all participants. This is not untypical when using on-line assessments, but does limit the process, and organisations need to work hard to educate staff on the purpose of such methods. Overall though as this is a new organisation the response levels were good and it is positive to note that most scores sit around the good (3) rather than satisfactory level (2).

Interestingly some participants average score reduced after the programme and these individuals have been provided with coaching support to help them move forward in constantly changing and pressurised roles. The 360° nature of the pre and post assessment raises peoples expectations of improved approaches and participants need to be ready to deliver against such expectations.

Figure 19 360° Impact of new learning for each participant Organisation E

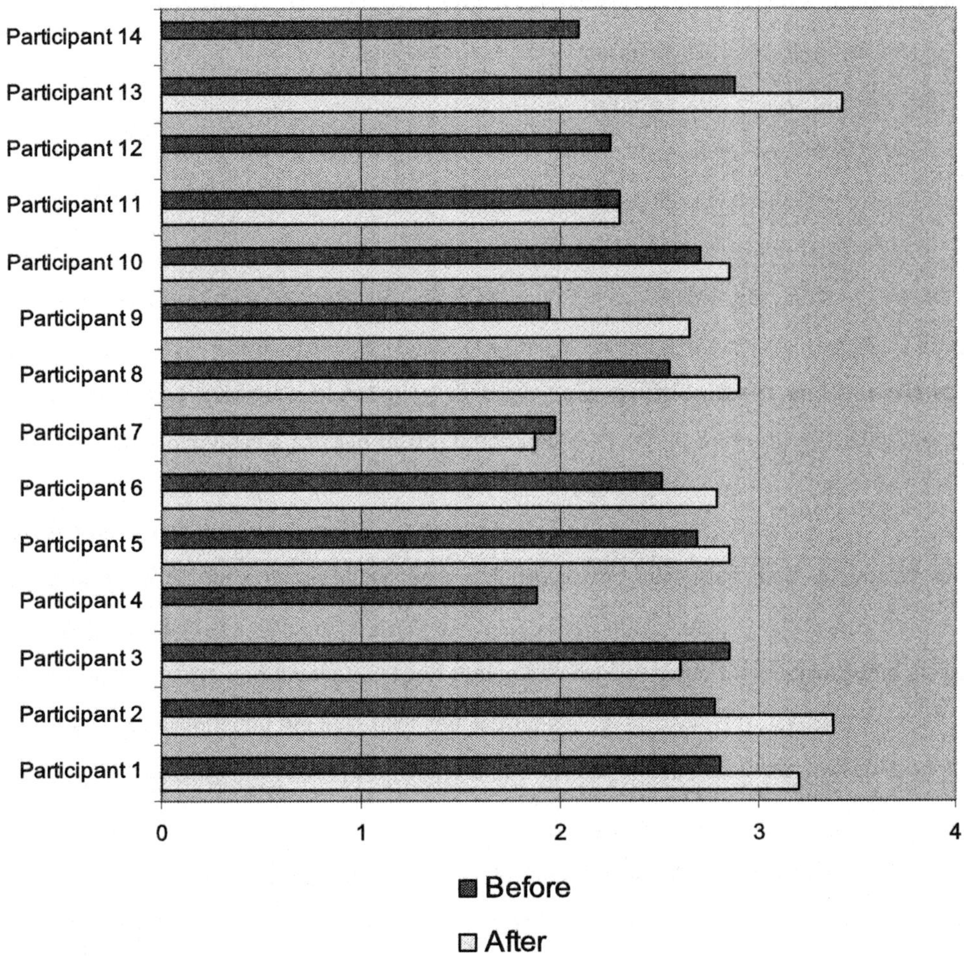

4	3	2	1
excellent	good	satisfactory	needs improvement

Organisational Impact

Figure 20 Participant self report on application of new learning Organisation E

I have been more pro-active in identifying & dealing with poor performance e.g. monitoring work/results. PDR reviews have helped me to do this and I have used regular one to one meetings as a platform to broach the subject with the staff concerned.
I am managing to delegate more effectively and am tackling some mild issues of poor performance. My progress has been patchy. Although a number of duties have been delegated, there are still one or two areas outstanding.
I set out to tackle poor performance and believe performance has improved in one particular area, although more time is needed to track this in results. We have a happy and well motivated team.
To delegate more in order to respond to increased volume of work and free up sometime to allow me to feel less stressed and to develop and empower my team. Allowed me to concentrate on new areas of work e.g. strategic and develop my team to gain new skills and motivate them.
My team has had the opportunity to add new skills and tasks to their CV. A regular supervision regime has been established that is tied in with job tasks and the team member's individual development plan. The advice team has taken on a role that's new to them and the organisation, so they are learning as they work.
We are starting to see a reduction in the number of times a customer rings to follow up on a reported repair, which is highlighting better customer service and higher standards. *Delegating more and managing poor performance more quickly has made us more efficient and this should result in savings for the organisation, although these are difficult to quantify.*

The level four measurement looked at the impact of the programme on the team, company and customers and identified the following improvements:

- A new website implemented
- Automation of invoice payments completed
- A more relaxed and confident approach to job roles
- Increased confidence in delegating work to teams
- Increased emphasis on leadership as opposed to management in the job role
- Enhanced project management skills

Return on Investment

Not all the results can be calculated as cash Return on Investment, although two participants were able to show how their actions reduced costs for the business. The cost savings were:

- £20,000 from a service level agreement for customer service provision
- £5,000 from the promotion of one of the programme participants

Using the established return on investment formula the ROI can be shown as:

$$\frac{\text{Benefit from training} - \text{cost of training} \times 100}{\text{Cost of training}} = \text{ROI\%}$$

$$\frac{\pounds 25000 - \pounds 15000 \times 100}{\pounds 15000} = 67\%$$

This was an encouraging result for the business and at this stage of their development, it proved very pleasing that their investment in improving their leaders could pay for itself via cost savings.

In conclusion

This is another example of a successful outcome that was achieved due to the ongoing commitment to the programme from the Senior Management Team. The Chief Executive often popped into the sessions to provide support and to check the programme was helping managers to achieve their objectives. This proved a big incentive to the participants who were also well supported by their line managers.

The strategic decision by the Chief Executive and Senior Team at the outset that all managers would go through the same programme was important, as this was seen as an opportunity for sharing and learning about the business as well as developing relationships, leadership and management skills.

The role of qualifications in reinforcing the learning cannot be underestimated. In this case, the participants completed the formal workshops over a six month period, had two study surgeries and submitted their work within ten months of starting. Whilst this may seem like a long timescale for an introductory award, it formed part of the transfer strategy, and it was clear from the examples submitted in the assignments that the learning was being positively implemented across the business.

A further group has now gone through the programme with a similar level of success, Organisation E is addressing its future talent management challenges and is now offering the programme with a few minor alterations to people who they perceive as tomorrow's managers and leaders.

CHAPTER 9

DEVELOPING TOMORROW'S LEADERS

Organisation F applied the Performance Improvement Cycle© to prepare team leaders and supervisors for management roles. Through this process key learning emerged on how ROI could be improved by small process changes

Background

Organisation F had decided to adopt a talent management process, for team leaders and supervisors who they believed had potential to take on more responsible roles. The Learning and Development Team approached us to help them by delivering a management development programme supported by the GPSVision Performance Improvement Cycle©. The overarching aim of the programme was to develop the participants into a more confident group, who could progress in the organisation to lead and motivate teams and deliver better performance.

Evaluation and Benchmarking

In this case it was difficult to identify higher level organisational objectives at the outset, due to the size and diversity of the organisation and participants were recruited from different divisions with very different roles. We therefore agreed to evaluate the learning outcomes (qualifications) and the success of individuals in securing promotions as the higher level objectives for the programme. To demonstrate individual contribution, participants were asked to design and complete a work based project.

Participants were asked to complete a 360° evaluation of skills prior to starting the programme, with colleagues, direct reports and managers giving feedback, to be repeated and reviewed six months after the last workshop was completed. The 360° questionnaire was supplemented by a number of self evaluation questionnaires against some of the job based requirements such as disciplinary and grievance practices, and recruitment and selection practices (see Figure 21)

Targets

All participants to complete the formal qualification and that there would be two promotions from the cohort within a year.

Intervention and Transfer

The programme chosen was the Level 4 Introductory Diploma in Management accredited by the Chartered Management Institute. Five full day sessions and two half day study support sessions were provided, plus significant formative feedback on assignments and projects provided.

To help in the transfer of learning, participants were asked to set personal goals and track their own progress and the resulting impact. Each was asked to complete a project initiation form and to progress their project, linking it to the learning from the programme. As some of the participants were unable to gain experience within their own role, we asked that line managers offered delegation opportunities.

Participants were registered as students with the CMI and they were required to complete a formal assignment demonstrating achievement of the learning outcomes. We encouraged the participants to use practical examples, supported with the relevant theory, as this demonstrated understanding of practice as well as principles.

Measurement and Evaluation

Reaction

The participants gave a positive set of reaction level evaluations stating that they were pleased with all five workshops and found the delivery style engaging and stimulating. The average score to the question around their ability to use the learning in the workplace was 4.1 out of 5. Whilst all reaction is important, this is the most important from an impact perspective.

Learning

Evidence of learning was evaluated by assessing the number of professional awards gained and the self evaluation exercise against procedural elements of the programme. (Figure 21)

Figure 21 Reported improvement of experience following programme Organisation F

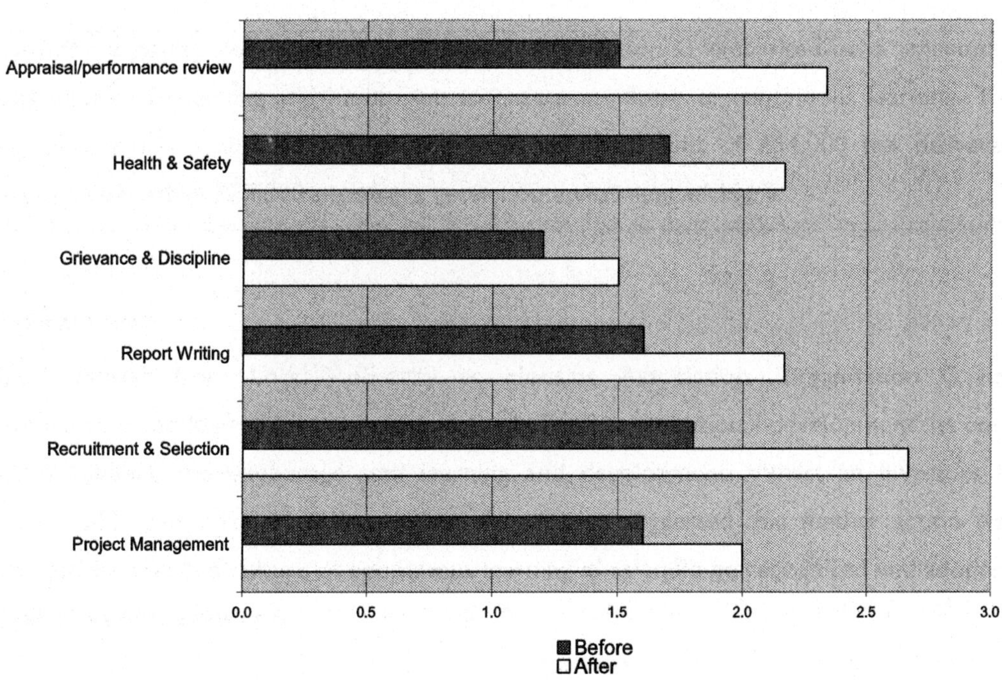

The numbers of participants who passed the qualification was used as evidence of learning. At the time of writing this case study of the twelve enrolled, the outcomes were:

Figure 22 Completion rates for qualification Organisation F

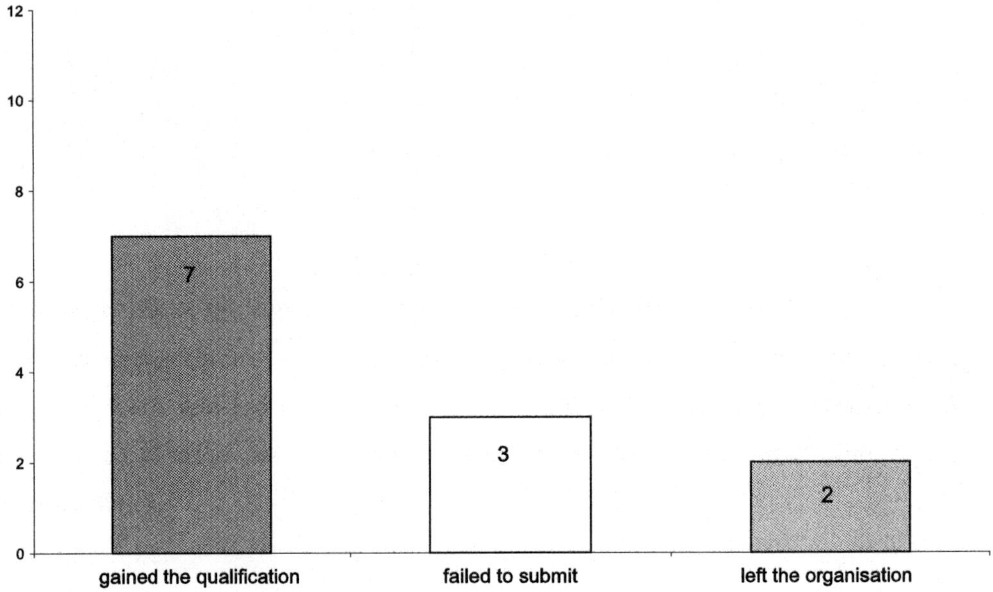

This was quite a disappointing completion rate and lower than many other accredited programmes. Our thoughts about this are included in the conclusions section at the end of the Chapter.

We also captured evidence of learning through post questionnaires and interviews and Figure 23 below provides a sample of the feedback:

Figure 23 Reported learning from CMI programme Organisation F

Developing good working relationships with colleagues and customers had an impact on the success of the project
How to structure, write and present a report taking into consideration the audience and purpose
Identifying Stakeholders and meeting their requirements
Planning and managing resources and projects (be aware of the resources available and legal requirements)
Setting up clear objectives that meet SMART criteria (Specific, Measurable, Achievable, Relevant and Time Related)
Recruitment and Selection: Importance of the Person Specification and Job description during the advertisement, short listing and interviewing processes
Promoting Quality and continuous improvements to the workplace and work practices

Participants CMI Introductory Diploma Organisation F

Behavioural change

The third level of measurement which looks at behavioural change shows increased performance against nineteen of the twenty areas assessed, which is a very positive result. (Figure 24)

Figure 24 360° Analysis before and after learning Organisation F

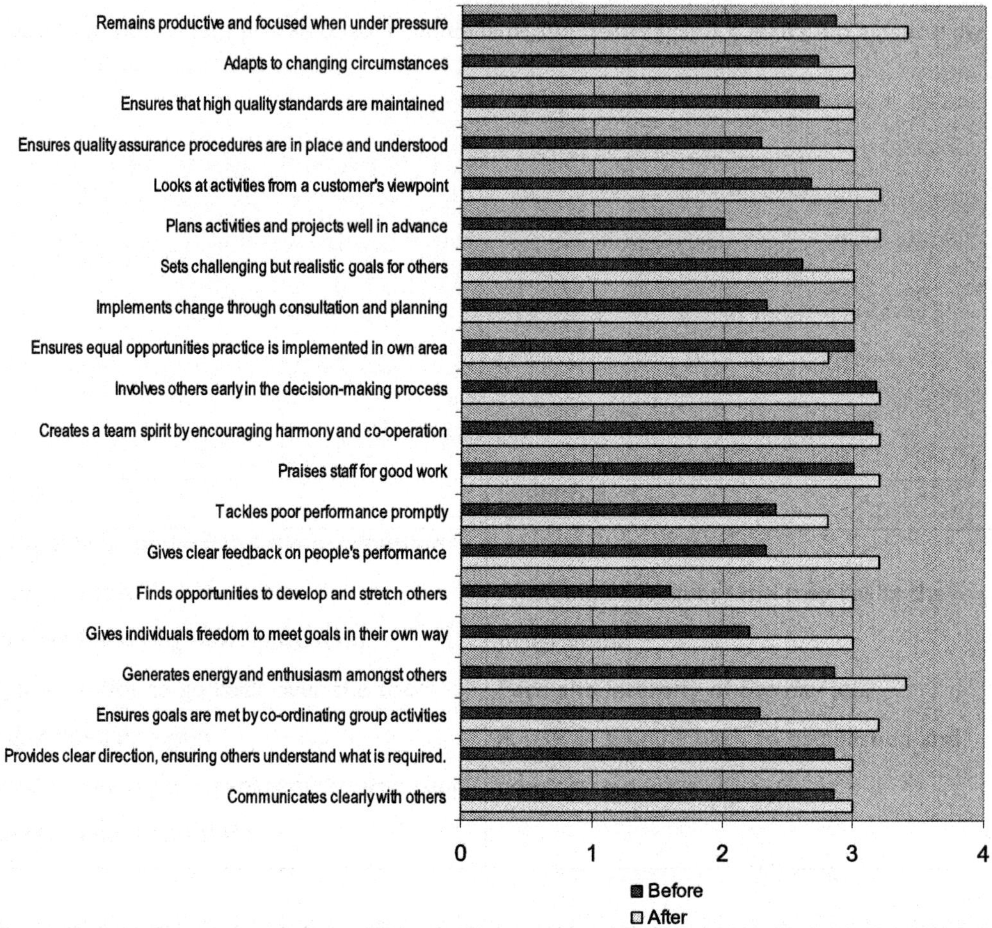

4	3	2	1
excellent	good	satisfactory	needs improvement

Significant improvements were recorded against:

- Finding opportunities to develop and stretch others
- Gives individuals freedom to meet goals in their own way
- Gives clear feedback on people's performance
- Planning activities and projects well in advance

Participants also provided evidence around their behavioural change as follows:

Figure 25 Behavioural change comments resulting from CMI programme Organisation F

The theoretical knowledge learned on the Introductory Diploma in Management course was put in practice and benefits were visible. I am more confident not only on planning and implementing a project but also on other aspects of my day to day job i.e. managing other staff, my development, recruitment process, legal requirements, delegating, empowering and motivating staff etc,
I have moved on from my current role into a leadership role and the programme has helped me to make changes to my work practices. My team has noticed a more mature person with an understanding of management protocols.

Organisational Impact

Level four measurement looks at the impact of the programme on the participant, team, company and customers. An impact questionnaire was circulated to the group but unfortunately only three participants responded to this. The results from this small group show:

- Improved staff morale
- Better patient care due to improved record keeping
- Focused activity due to better management information
- Increased knowledge and better management skills

Figure 26 Self reports to impact from CMI programme Organisation F

Staff have worked towards putting good systems in place to quickly deal with any data quality issues and day to day running of the office.
Patient care has improved as we have more clinical time as the data inputting is completed by a data input clerk.
Monthly activity reports facilitate the monitoring of performance for each service and allow steps to be taken when performance needs to be improved or service needs to be developed/expanded.
I have a wider knowledge of management skills and practical based solutions.

The Organisational Development Manager was pleased that most participants had gained a recognised management qualification, but disappointed that others had chosen not to submit the written work.

Return on investment

The programme cost £9,500 to run and resulted in the promotion of two people which can be converted into cash ROI. The CIPD figures for 2008 shows a cost of £5,000 to recruit staff at this level. Using this data alone the programme would have paid for itself with net savings of £10,000 generated. There are other improvements that could possibly be converted to a business saving but the organisation is happy to leave these as intangible benefits.

$$\frac{\text{Benefit from training} - \text{cost of training} \times 100}{\text{Cost of training}} = \text{ROI\%}$$

$$\frac{£10000 - £9500 \times 100}{£9500} = 5\%$$

In conclusion

Participants reacted very well to the programme, so no specific changes were proposed to the format or content of the programme. However a number of areas were identified that would have improved the effectiveness of the programme and the ease of capturing ROI.

Participants' line managers must be willing and able to:

- Provide opportunities for participants to change
- Provide flexibility to try out new approaches
- Provide support to help embed their new learning
- Provide time and support to encourage completing the qualification

Increased emphasis needs to be placed on identifying barriers to applying the learning within the work place at the outset as some managers stated they were unable to apply their learning and the transfer due to the workplace environment.

The self evaluation for each participant shows some positive and some disappointing information. Only four of the twelve participants completed the questionnaire before and after the programme. This level of response by the participants to the questionnaires demonstrates clearly the culture described by Darling. [xviii] We believe this was due to a lack of understanding of the process and a perception that the workshops were the cornerstone of the programme rather than just one other part of the learning process. One of the key issues impacting upon this group of learners was the constantly changing structures and targets within the NHS which adds additional work pressures and can lead to a negative effect on morale.

Programme aims need to be more specific and measurable. Converting goals to cash is easier if the monetary value of some of these points is known at the outset. It is helpful where programme aims have metrics attached to them. Alternatively nationally accepted notional data and/or average hourly rates could be used to calculate efficiencies or time saved.

The low rate of completion of the award was a disappointment to us. Our experience in Organisation A and Organisation E gave us a high completion rate of coursework (85%). Completion here was actively encouraged by the Senior Management Teams, which motivated the learners. We now recommend to all our customers that if accredited programmes are chosen, then the qualification should be seen as a mandatory part of the learning programme.

CHAPTER 10

LEARNING THROUGH COACHING

Following a review for Investors in People, Organisation G embarked on a structured programme of coaching and mentoring to create a culture of continuous learning. The organisation has embraced change and from an investment of £34,000 has delivered savings in excess of £87,000 showing a return on investment of 156%.

Background

Since transfer from Local Authority to Housing Association, Organisation G has demonstrated an impressive commitment to staff and organisational development. Its core values support and encourage staff learning and development. Whilst an Investors in People (IiP) review report acknowledged this, it also suggested that further action was required to 'create a culture of continuous learning' that could be recognised and adopted by all areas of the business.

Evaluation and Benchmarking

The IiP report identified a need to improve management development activities and recommended a more structured approach to coaching and mentoring as part of this development process.

The organisation recognised a culture had developed where individuals expected managers to be directive, leading to low empowerment of employees. The result of this was that managers spent much of their time organising others work, solving common problems and answering queries. This gave them less time for their own work, and gave rise to a phenomenon sometimes know as "acting down", i.e. doing the work of your subordinates because this makes life easier.

Although much of the evidence was anecdotal, there was a general view at a senior level that a coaching culture would improve organisational performance. Senior and middle managers were selected as the target group initially, although the organisation has now gone on to cascade the development programme down to all staff with supervisory responsibilities.

Benchmarking of individuals was completed through a 360° coaching skills analysis covering the range of skills involved in the coaching process.

Targets

It took some time to identify the specific outcomes that could be demonstrated from this programme. After a number of meetings with the Organisational Development Director and a selection of participants the following targets were agreed:

- Staff at all levels taking more personal responsibility for managing their work, dealing with problems and coming up with more effective ways of working
- More problem solving approaches used at team and individual level to help to improve processes and facilitate change
- Managers using coaching as a development technique with all staff
- Managers using coaching to address performance issues
- All staff recognising that a coaching approach has a broader application and can be used with customers, suppliers, peers and senior colleagues
- Managers empowering staff to take appropriate decisions without consultation freeing up managerial time for priority activity
- Reduced conflict within and between teams and individuals

Intervention and Transfer

The programme was designed to run in three phases, to mirror the preparation, intervention and embedding model.

A half day Induction session provided context for the programme and an introduction to some of the key concepts around the Learning Organisation (Pedlar and Burgoyne [xix] Senge 1994) [xx] and some of the key definitions of coaching.

The programme continued with two full day workshops covering the key content:

- Communication skills for coaching
- The Grow model
- Problem solving techniques
- One to one coaching interventions
- Team coaching
- Delegation and empowerment

Four half-day reflective learning sessions were used to support the two formal workshops with the aim of embedding the learning. These were restricted to a maximum of eight people to encourage discussion around application levels and action learning sets. This changed the nature of the learning process quite significantly and whilst quite a radical shift from traditional learning approaches, proved to be very effective.

At the Induction session participants were invited to anticipate what would enable or inhibit the application of new skills. Their results have been collated and summarised as follows:

Enablers	Inhibitors
Being able to understand the programme Time to apply the new ideas Support for trying new approaches Opportunities to go back over the tools and techniques again Need to see higher management practising the techniques and skills	Avoiding colleagues who may resist the programme Pace and intensity of the day job A risk of slipping back to established and comfortable ways

This data was circulated to the senior management team to ensure they encouraged the enablers and reduced the chance of inhibitors affecting the programme.

Measurement and Evaluation

Reaction

The participants gave a positive reaction in their evaluation of the programme stating that they were pleased with all workshops and found the mix between a traditional workshop style and reflective learning sessions engaging and relevant.

Learning

The sessions involved a lot of practical work around participants own 360° results, with this data being used to facilitate practical coaching sessions. In addition they brought current operational issues to the sessions and used a range of analytical tools including Fishbone[xxi], Six Thinking Hats[xxii] and Force Field[xxiii] models to progress these.

During the progress of the first cohort of learners, we discussed the possibility with Organisation G of accrediting the work with the Chartered Management Institute, who had recently introduced a number of Coaching and Mentoring qualifications.

As a result the Level 5 qualification in Management Coaching and Mentoring has now been introduced and for subsequent cohorts has become a mandatory part of the course. To date ninety participants have enrolled for the qualification and 48 have completed and received a Level 5 Award in Management Coaching and Mentoring.

We have now dedicated one of the follow up sessions to assignment development, and we hold sessions in a computer suite where people can either start or continue to work on their assignments. This approach has been particularly successful with increased numbers of participants finishing their assignments within agreed timescales.

Participant learning comments include:

I found the chance to reflect on the context of the programme useful.

Reflecting on how models could be used was helpful and agreeing shorter but smarter objectives will help my team.

The GROW model was particularly useful but I am also using the thinking hats model.

We used one of the coaching tools (six hats) to look at my project and this helped me in confirming my thought process and also added a little to my SWOT analysis.

Participants Organisation G

Behavioural Change

Pre and post 360 degree questionnaires were used to assess the levels of behavioural change, against the twenty seven assessed areas of competence. The results from the participants, their line managers, their colleagues and direct reports are shown in Figure 27. It is positive to note that there have been improvements in twenty six of the twenty seven areas. Significant progress being made against the following competences:

- Uses appropriate techniques when questioning, bearing in mind the needs of the learner and of the task in hand
- Gains commitment and acceptance to performance goals
- Ensures that goals are SMART
- Encourages learners to accept responsibility for their own development by agreeing an appropriate Performance Development Plan
- Demonstrates patience
- Is reflective and analytical
- Communicates a belief in the potential of people to improve performance
- Acts as a positive role model

Figure 27 360° coaching skills analysis before and after Organisation G

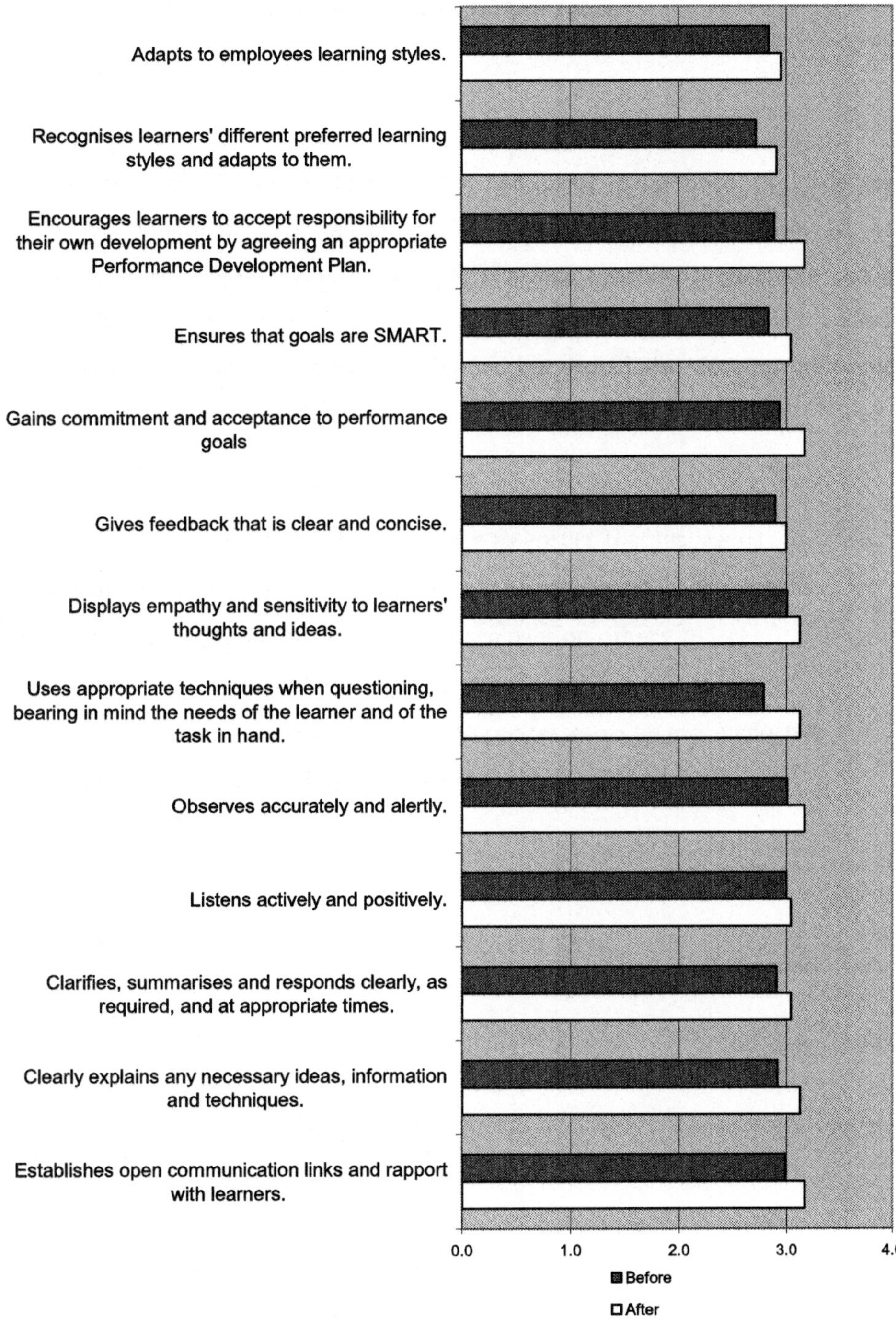

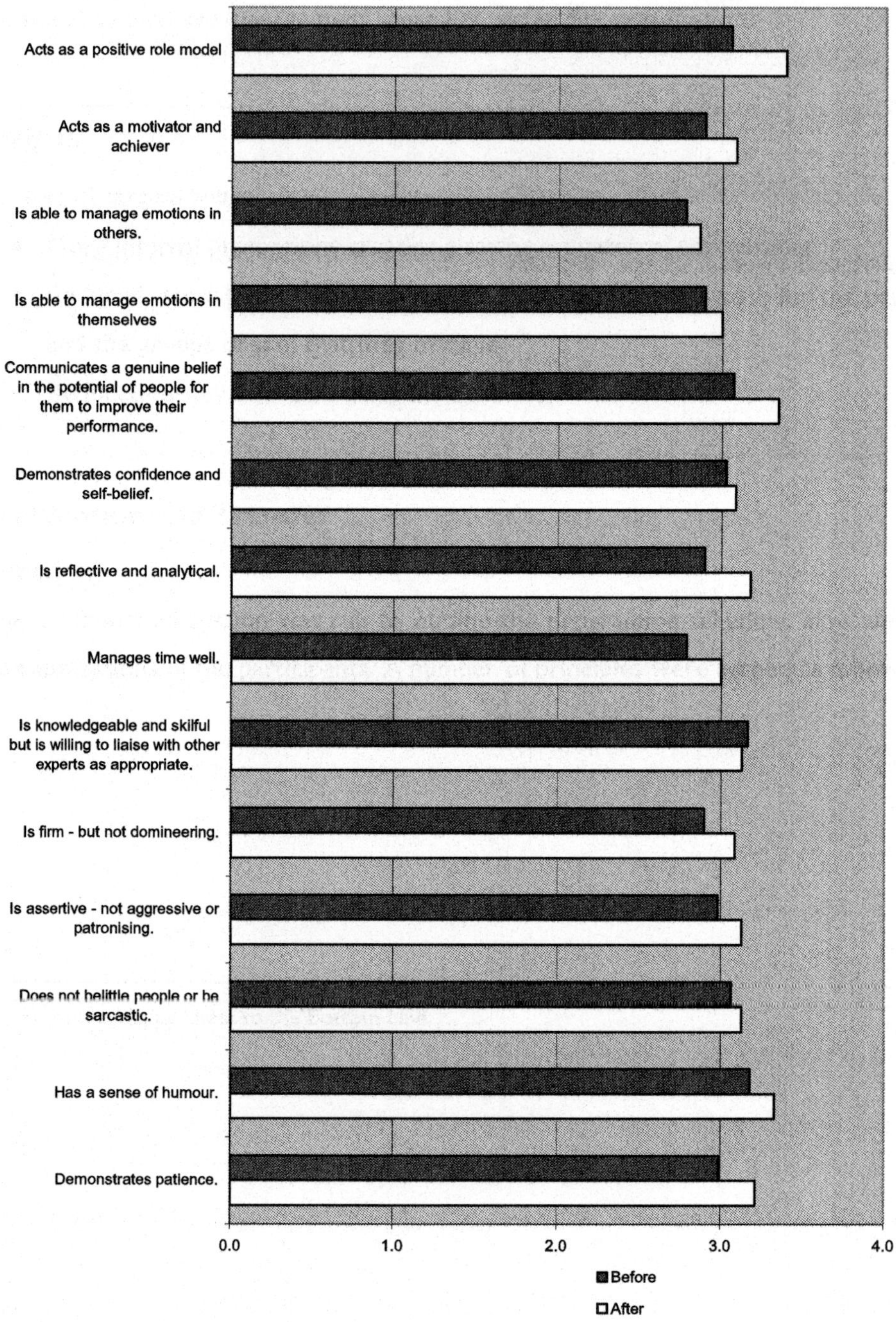

4	3	2	1	0
Exceptional	Fully Effective	Developing	Development needs identified	I can't evaluate this, or no answer

This is a positive set of results, and particularly pleasing as they have been validated by line managers, colleagues and staff. This evidence has helped the organisation to continue on its mission of developing a continuous learning culture and has been shared at numerous award ceremonies.

Organisational Impact

Managers were invited to provide feedback on how they have used the programme to make an impact on their teams, organisation and customers. A sample of the feedback from managers is set out below with an example against the seven target areas identified at the beginning of the programme.

Staff at all levels taking more personal responsibility for managing their work, dealing with problems and coming up with more effective ways of working
My goal was to resolve relationship issues between two of my staff. Adopting a "can do" coaching approach has removed the issue of me constantly having to "look for the solution" and has taken away any emotion, worry or concern I had about managing the situation. My approach with them has saved time as the issue is no longer a point of discussion in our 1-to-1 meetings. Productivity levels have increased and although initially they were reluctant to take on greater responsibility, they have taken on their role with enthusiasm, with occasional blips along the way.

More problem solving approaches used at team and individual level to help to improve processes and facilitate change
My goal was to introduce my team to the problem solving models, develop them as a problem solving unit and develop the problem solving capabilities of individual team members. So far the results have been very positive. Morale in the team has improved, in some areas more than others, and there is generally a better attitude towards achieving targets.

Managers using coaching as a development tool with all staff
I set myself a goal to ask more questions and make better use of 1-to-1 meetings through using coaching techniques and models in practical work and team scenarios. *I set myself a goal to demonstrate to a team member that they have the scope, skills and capacity to break some of their own perceptions of their capabilities. They have developed their own self confidence through my positive feedback and have taken on more responsibility.*

Managers using coaching to address performance issues
My goal was to address some negative behaviours and fit of a particular team member. The Individual has made significant improvements in their approach and is now recognised as a key member of the team. We have delivered a programme that is setting good practice and achieving results with a difficult client group.

All staff recognising that a coaching approach has a broader application and can be used with customers, suppliers, peers and senior colleagues

I'm more relaxed since the coaching programme and as a result the team seems more positive and happy in what they are doing. This is delivering higher productivity, reduced costs, plus some of the initiatives we have worked on have improved communication with customers, and allowed us to give a better service in general.

I used my coaching skills in a training programme around data protection. The programme was entered for an Award due to the method of training used and we have more employees aware of Data Protection and the serious implications that can occur from not protecting data correctly. Customer data is now taken more seriously and hopefully employees will respect this, thus maintaining our professional reputation.

Managers empowering staff to take appropriate decisions without consultation freeing up managerial time for priority activity

My goal was to delegate more and develop my team to take more ownership of their roles and responsibilities. This would allow me to concentrate on my project type work and develop my role and experience beyond finance.
It has given me more time to get involved with non finance projects and grow my knowledge and experience. I have recognised that I don't need to know every detail as I have a team that does and this makes me feel more relaxed and approachable.

Reduced conflict within and between teams and individuals
I have a great example arising from some tension which had existed between one of my managers and another service manager. I explored with my manager what her concerns were, and asked her to go to the third perspective, to think about the impact of how she preferred to deal with a problem, and to identifying and consider using different approaches to building relationships. It has been a great success, despite some initial scepticism from my manager. *I believe this has led to a better atmosphere within the team and everyone feels valued and knows their role. A real spin off has been 100% attendance by 4 of my 5 team members with only 4 days off for the person that was ill. These are the best absence figures we have ever achieved and we were nominated for Team of the Year in 2008.*

Return on Investment

A range of positive outcomes were generated including:

- More time being spent on thinking positively rather than spending time on explaining what hasn't happened or why the problem is someone else's.
- No overspend on reactive repairs. This is partly due to the better relationship between finance and the craft workers.
- One manager has been promoted since commencing the programme
- An audio CD was produced for £250 rather than the usual cost of £1500
- The new client information system has saved the IT department 8 days work per annum
- Three managers felt that improved departmental working relationships have helped to reduce staff turnover in their departments by almost 2%

It is not easy to convert some of these improvements to cash but the CIPD (Chartered Institute of Professional Development) averages for 2008 data prove helpful. They show the average cost to recruit is £5,000 and the average cost of one person leaving a company is £5,800. We can therefore show

- A saving of £5,000 for the promotion
- Reduced staff turnover has delivered savings of £81,200 (£5,800 x 14 employees).
- Time savings at £15 per hour for 8 days at 7.5 hours equates to £900

$$\frac{\text{Benefit from training} - \text{cost of training} \times 100}{\text{Cost of training}} = \text{ROI\%}$$

$$\frac{£87100 - £34000 \times 100}{£34000} = 156\%$$

In conclusion

Developing a culture change programme needs to be very carefully planned and should involve a number of champions and stakeholders to ensure a smooth implementation process.

Line managers need to be encouraged to provide practical opportunities for their staff to apply the new learning and remain open to new approaches and ideas.

The process gained momentum as it began to filter down into the organisation.

Teach the participants that the results will not be seen overnight, but they will see a gradual shift in approach.

Persisting with capturing ROI data has shown that this programme can pay for itself from savings made.

CHAPTER 11

PERFORMANCE COACHING

Organisation H wanted to support senior managers through challenging times. A coaching approach was sought to build on previous learning and provide operational support around a range of personal and work based challenges. This approach developed significant tangible and intangible benefits to the organisation including savings of £124,000 against an investment of £52,000 generating a ROI of 138%.

Background

Many managers were well qualified; many had prior experience of leadership and management development programmes. To gain greater impact from its leaders, Organisation H developed a one to one performance coaching programme and offered places on the basis of a written application. This approach was to build a sustainable programme, as it would offer individual support, but would also develop the participants coaching skills, so that it would have a wider impact within the organisation.

Evaluation and Benchmarking

The key aims of the coaching programme were to ensure that managers:

- Understand their roles and responsibilities in managing and leading others
- Reflect on their style and behaviour and its impact on others
- Can delegate effectively and empower others
- Use a range of management techniques and processes to be more effective
- Deal with conflict confidently and promptly

At the beginning of the programme all participants undertook two individual benchmarking exercises, one was a 360° skills analysis and the other an APTER™ Motivational Styles Profile (AMSP)[xxiv] to identify motivational states experienced by the candidates.

The organisation recognised that line managers were struggling to balance their time between the task, the team and their staff. The sheer volume of work, continuous change and shift in direction was hampering managers in their need to support their teams. As a result the coaching programme was designed to provide more individual support to reduce stress, offer options for dealing with problems, to consider own development needs and to improve management capability within the organisation.

Targets

The formal targets were:

- More internal promotions creating a saving on external recruitment
- Reduced stress levels leading to reduced sickness absence, both for the participants and the groups of staff that they manage
- Reduced turnover levels across the business

Intervention and Transfer

Induction

A group induction session was run to outline the programme schedule, aims and identify the expectations of the participants. A number of principles were agreed as follows:

- Listening is vitally important
- Everyone is capable of achieving more
- A person's past is no indication of their future
- People's beliefs about what is possible for themselves are their only limits
- A coach always provides support
- Coaches don't provide the answers
- Coaching will involve constructive feedback
- Confidentiality is guaranteed
- Some situations cannot be helped by coaching

The focus of the programme was management coaching, and we introduced concepts, theories, models and ideas to participants to help them with their leadership and management skills, thus providing a differential from life coaching or counselling.

After the induction, each participant attended a one-to-one coaching session each month for the period of a year. Initial coaching sessions involved using the AMSP psychometric tool and the 360° evaluation to identify positives and areas to challenge. As is the nature with coaching, following the initial diagnostic phase, each participant chose to work on their own agenda with the help of their coach. Some of these included:

• Being more assertive • Time management • Managing difficult staff • Structuring teams • Managing your manager • Workload survival • Political behaviour	• Job application including interview prep • Preparing for Performance Review • Applying for further training and development • Strategies to achieve required outcomes • Managing your own motivational state reversals

Measurement and Evaluation

Reaction

Reaction level evaluation was gathered from participants responding to questionnaires and feedback received by the coaches. Twenty six managers received coaching during the programme with a typical duration of 12 to15 months.

Feedback comments included:

> *This is the best training I have ever had*
>
> *Coaching in my case has made me realise my own potential*
>
> *I responded well to the non judgemental and listening approach used by the coach*
>
> *I am looking forward with more confidence and assertiveness now, which is mostly due to the support received from the coaching sessions*
>
> Participants Organisation H

Learning

Figure 28 Competency Self Assessment Organisation H

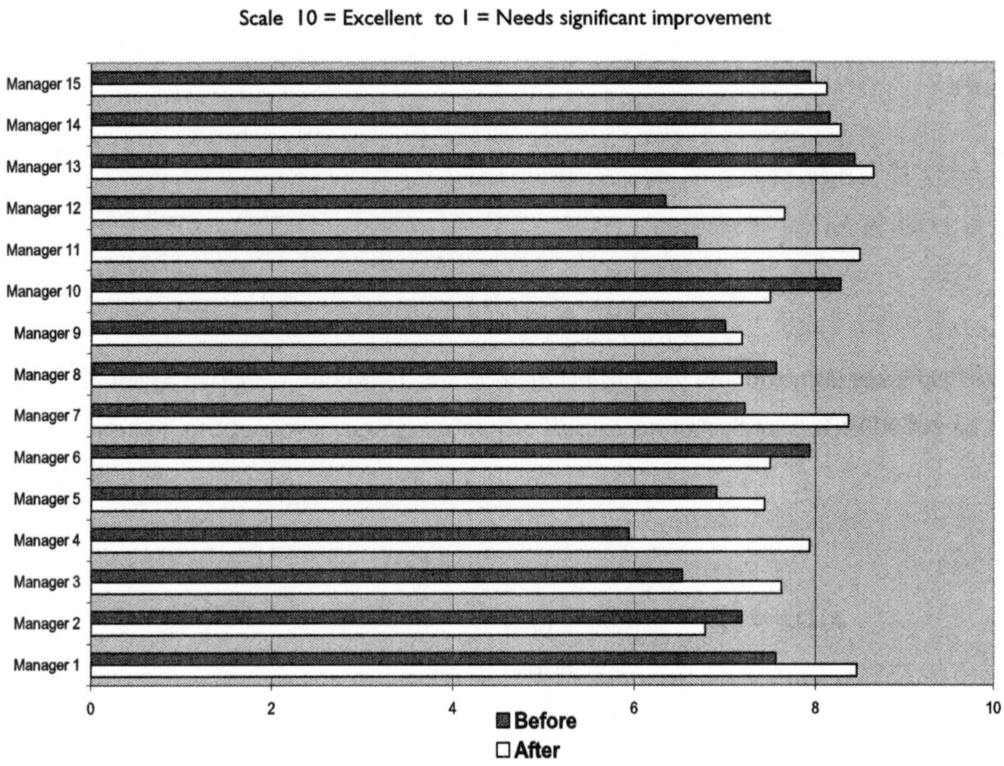

This compares the results before and after the programme. An interesting observation is that four participants gave themselves a lower score after the programme. An analysis of this highlighted that these participants learned that they were less skilled than they originally thought or now have a more realistic view of their knowledge and skills. Another factor we have discovered is that some participants are nervous of self evaluation at the start of a programme and therefore can overestimate their scores.

Unfortunately not all participants completed both the pre and post questionnaire so we are only able to show the results for 15 participants. However it was pleasing to note that eleven participants showed improved scores after the programme.

Behavioural Change

The third level of measurement looked at behavioural change using an APTER motivational styles psychometric review and a repeat of the 360° benchmarking questionnaire.

APTER Motivational Styles Profile review

In addition to the competence based 360 degree questionnaire, the APTER motivational styles psychometric questionnaire was used as a benchmarking tool before the programme began. The diagnostic analysed the time that the participants spent in the different states and the results were reviewed during the first coaching session with development plans agreed.

State	Purpose	State	Purpose
Serious	Progress and achievement	Playful	Fun and enjoyment, being in the moment
Conforming	Fitting in and doing things right	Rebellious	Challenging and creating change
Mastery	Power and control	Sympathy	Relationships and nurturing
Self	Responsibility and self focus	Other	Looking to others' needs

The AMSP is based around the principles of Reversal Theory, which encourages participants to look at which styles they adopt in particular situations and how this affects their outcomes. The post phase asked them to reflect on any goals they set for themselves as a result of the report findings. The following is a collection of their goals and reflection on their personal achievements:

I recognised I was spending very little time in the self state and this was affecting my ability to manage my time well. I addressed this by making use of MS Outlook, task and calendar functions to assist with designating blocks of time for clearly designated tasks, thereby helping me to achieve what was required in a structured and time efficient manner, without the associated stress of being disorganised. I no longer use a paper diary as all daily activity is recorded in Outlook and I bought my own PDA to help me function when not at my desk.

I set out to reduce the time I spend in the playful state as I felt it was affecting my ability to get some staff to achieve their results. I identified that it is not always necessary to be everyone's "friend" and that, in fact; it sometimes loses respect from others. I have tried to be much more assertive with this team and gain their respect by demonstrating that, as their manager, they need to realise that my decisions are often based on service needs and not on individuals.

I recognised that I was not spending enough time in the mastery state and I found it difficult to challenge people or stand up for what I felt. I needed to be able to challenge on a professional basis and although I have developed my skills and confidence to challenge more easily I remain unable to "switch off" and still take concerns home. I will continue to work on this style as I believe it will help me to become more objective and take feedback more objectively rather than as criticism.

I needed to spend less time in the rebellious state as I would often adopt a knee jerk reaction to situations which could create disruption within the team. My style was not encouraging team working and I needed to sit back from the situation and encourage the team to work through the issues/problems and develop solutions themselves. I have made some progress here but need to keep working on this area.

I was overly serious and did not have very good work/life balance and therefore didn't particularly enjoy work or home. I needed more boundaries around work and life and aimed to work more predictable hours and to leave work more often at the right time and to make time for activities at home. As a result I am feeling more in control at work and enjoying my free time much more.

I was too rebellious and inclined to express myself in an overly emotional way rather than in a controlled way and could come across as disruptive and challenging to others. I could hear myself in this mode in the first few sessions with my coach. I set out to communicate in a more constructive manner and hold back from expressing feelings. I have managed to successfully contest some issues with line manager and peers, which previously may have ended in a direct argument with a "because I said so"- type conclusion.

I increased the time I spent in the mastery state as I was guilty of failing to forward plan and failing to prepare for meetings. My progress has been excellent and I now research the agenda and arrive on time for meetings. I now delegate the role of chair and minute taker, opposed to taking on these roles myself. There is an increased level of buy- in by staff within the department and more ownership of subjects/work areas.

Figure 29 360° results Organisation H

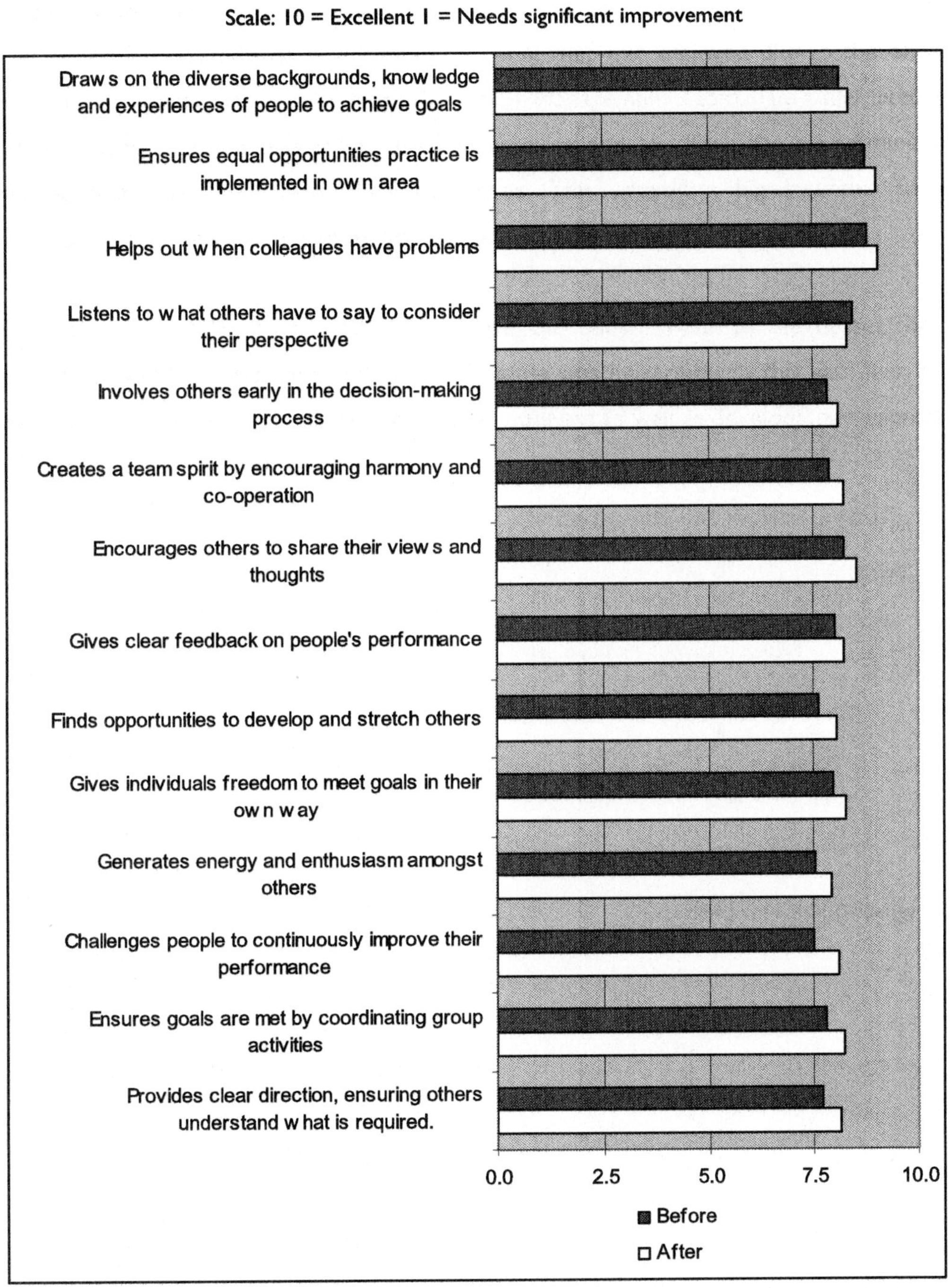

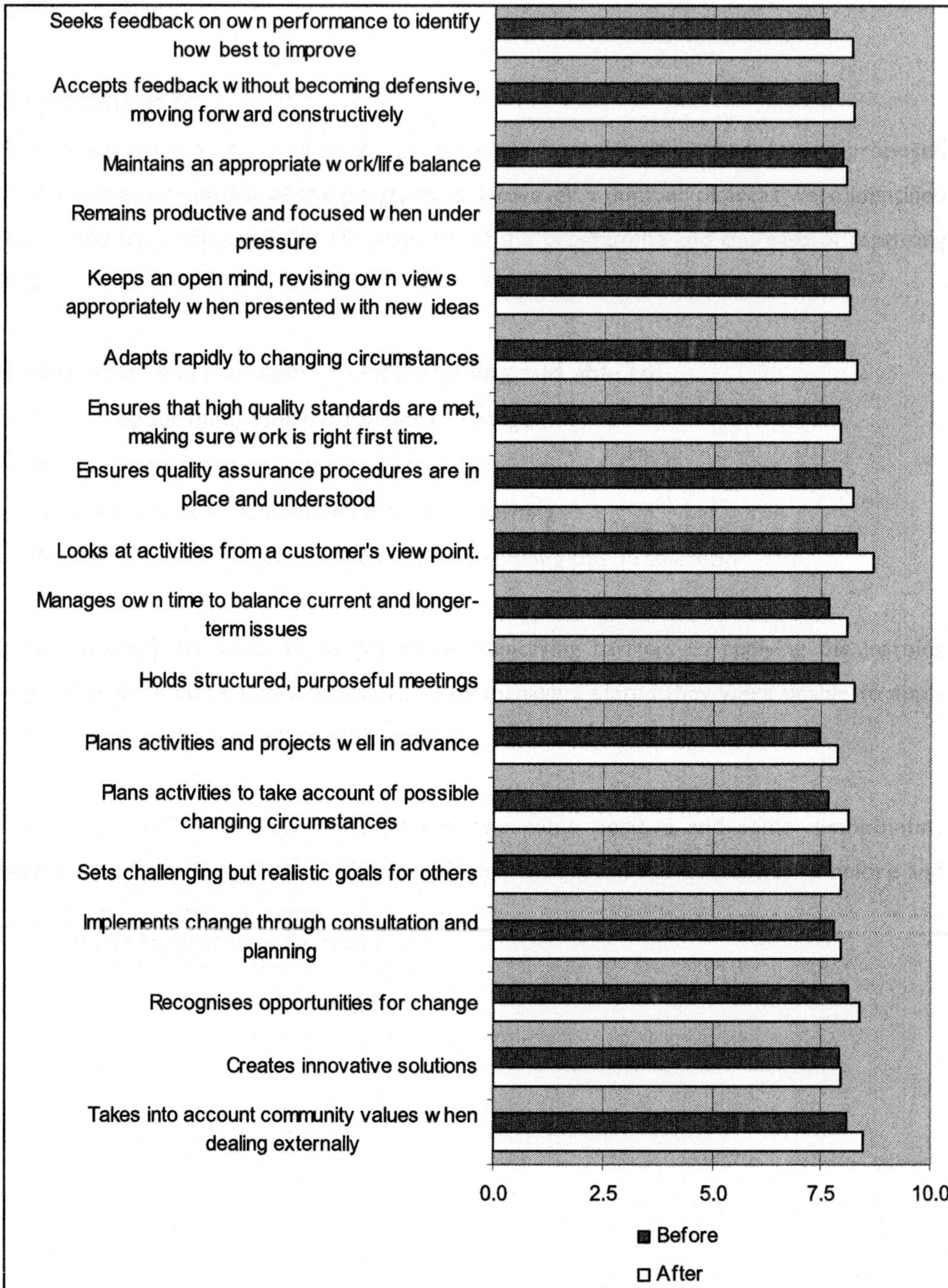

Seeks feedback on own performance to identify how best to improve
Accepts feedback without becoming defensive, moving forward constructively
Maintains an appropriate work/life balance
Remains productive and focused when under pressure
Keeps an open mind, revising own views appropriately when presented with new ideas
Adapts rapidly to changing circumstances
Ensures that high quality standards are met, making sure work is right first time.
Ensures quality assurance procedures are in place and understood
Looks at activities from a customer's viewpoint.
Manages own time to balance current and longer-term issues
Holds structured, purposeful meetings
Plans activities and projects well in advance
Plans activities to take account of possible changing circumstances
Sets challenging but realistic goals for others
Implements change through consultation and planning
Recognises opportunities for change
Creates innovative solutions
Takes into account community values when dealing externally
0.0
2.5
5.0
7.5
10.0
Before
After

Significant progress was made by participants in:

- Focusing and engaging my team on goal achievement
- Behaving assertively when pressed
- Developing innovative skills in the team
- Leading from the front with more structure and planning time built into my work

Organisational Impact

The improvements highlighted by the participants, their line managers, staff and colleagues have led to improvements in how they manage their teams. Higher scores include:

- Challenges people to continuously improve their performance
- Plans activities and projects well in advance
- Holds structured, purposeful meetings
- Manages own time to balance current and longer-term issues
- Looks at activities from a customer's viewpoint
- Remains productive and focused when under pressure
- Seeks feedback on own performance to identify how best to improve

These points include a good mix of planning, organising, staff development, resilience, and personal development. Comments from participants around organisational impact include:

> *My team moans less and this means that patients have a better experience. The organisation could benefit from less complaints and a more positive regard for the hospital in general.*
>
> *We are seeing more patients than ever and have delivered a 5% cost improvement on the site and contributed to the Trust making a surplus at year end.*
>
> Coaching participants Organisation H

Return on Investment

The final level of measurement is a cash return on investment against the £52,000 invested in the programme. Savings have been identified via recruitment and labour turnover savings.

Additionally a number of participants cited the following impacts which have not been converted to cash. The client was delighted with these results and the fit with the original targets.

> *We have delivered a 5% cost improvement on the site (cash releasing) and contributed to the Trust making a surplus at year end.*
> *I am more focused now so I am spending more time on work that is of value to the organisation and patients.*
> *We save more bed days due to reducing the length of stays.*
> *Improvement in my confidence as a manager has resulted in being more assertive around local budget issues that should lead to longer term efficiency savings.*
>
> Coaching participants Organisation H

Ten participants felt the coaching programme helped them cope during the year and without this support they would have left the business. Using CIPD 2008 figures for turnover at this level of £10,000 per person, this has produced a saving of £100,000.

Four participants have been promoted during the programme and using the CIPD 2008 figures for recruiting managers at this level of £6,000, this shows a saving of £24,000.

These two achievements have saved £124,000 which when shown against the cost of the programme provides a positive ROI of 138%.

There are many intangible outcomes of this exercise that are still being assessed but using the recruitment and turnover savings alone the Return on Investment of 138% has so far been generated.

$$\frac{\text{Benefit from training} - \text{cost of training} \times 100}{\text{Cost of training}} = \text{ROI\%}$$

$$\frac{£124000 - £52000 \quad \times 100}{£52000} = 138\%$$

In conclusion

The NHS is a very challenging place for managers to work. The mix of external and internal change, coupled with many geographical bases, different populations and a hugely diverse staff mix adds to the complexity. The level of change that we have observed within the sector is at times bewildering and the sector seems to be in a constant of flux.

Each participant selected personal targets to work towards and each needed different types of support from their coach. With this type of programme, we recognise that group results may be less important than progress against individual benchmark and targets.

The level of line management support is recognised as a weakness, so in subsequent coaching cohorts we have introduced a joint coaching session with the line manager and participant present. This is designed to explore how the line manager can support the individual during the coaching programme. This has had some success although it has been difficult to track down more senior managers whose schedules appear to be fairly unmanageable.

Line managers will be encouraged to arrange three monthly sessions to review the goal setting progress and all coachees are expected to complete pre and post work around the 360° and profiling questionnaires.

With future programmes, Line managers will now attend session three which should increase their understanding and engagement levels.

We need to encourage coachees to think about return on investment and how some of their achievements can return cash savings or increased revenue to the business.

CHAPTER 12

KEY LEARNING POINTS

Organisation A

Setting clear targets is vital to being able to measure the outcomes at the end of a programme. If organisations performance indicators are transparent and clear to everyone it is far more likely that Return on Investment can be identified.

Some of the questions that need to be asked are:

- What is the business objective?
- What are the issues we need to address?
- What are the targets we need to set for individuals, teams, customers and the business?
- What is the appropriate learning intervention?
- What should the learning transfer strategy include?
- What timescales should be set around the process and evaluation plan?

Organisation B

It is important to take into account the learners' preferences for learning and their past learning experiences. It is also important to check the learners' expectations as this will increase engagement levels and the application of new skills.

In this example, the submission of assignments was variable with only 50% of participants gaining the qualification. Part of the problem here was the level of change that was going on at the time. The programme was intended to facilitate that change, but it is clear that the level of commitment required to complete the assignment was a step too far for some.

In future projects of this kind we would build in more assessment support during the workshops and encourage line managers to become more involved in this area.

Organisation C

We recognised the importance of real projects in helping to establish the Return on Investment from a training programme. Participants had to plan, manage and report on a chosen project, and were asked to present this to an audience which included the Senior Management Team of the Division.

All of the projects delivered significant improvements to service as well as cost savings and while some were very simple to evaluate in cash terms, others could be measured in terms of quality rather than quantity. It is important to be able to identify intangible as well as tangible outputs.

Another important factor was the commitment of Senior Management within this division to the programme. They had identified people who they believed could be stretched and would add significant value to the Division. They enhanced the value of the learning by staying close to the programme and by offering a lot of support to participants. Our experience has taught us that when 'programme champions' disengage or lose interest the impact results are greatly reduced.

Organisation D

The Third Sector was previously known as the Voluntary Sector, made up of charitable and not-for-profit organisations. Over the last twenty years, this sector has become increasingly businesslike, and has taken on responsibility for much service provision in areas such as social care, that was previously carried out by the public sector.

The result of this has been a growth in organisations competing for funding, needing to demonstrate excellence in practice and business skills. To meet this challenge, it is vital that not only professional and technical, but leadership and management skills are in place. In this case it was a vision of the Chief Executive who recognised the need to improve leadership and management skills across the organisation.

The decision was made not to accredit the programme and in retrospect we believe that this was a mistake. Generally we find accredited programmes provide a useful stage in the validation of learning and by forcing the participant to reflect, this increases their content retention levels. This increased level of retention gives participants more chance of applying their new learning which ultimately leads to increased behavioural change and Return on Investment.

Organisation E

This is another example of a successful outcome that was achieved due to the ongoing commitment to the programme from the Senior Management Team. The Chief Executive often popped into the sessions to provide support and to check the programme was helping managers to achieve their objectives. This proved a big incentive to the participants who were also well supported by their line managers.

The strategic decision by the Chief Executive and Senior Team at the outset that all managers would go through the same programme was important, as this was seen as an opportunity for sharing and learning about the business as well as developing relationships, leadership and management skills.

The role of qualifications in reinforcing the learning cannot be underestimated. In this case, the participants completed the formal workshops over a six month period, had two study surgeries and submitted their work within ten months of starting. Whilst this may seem like a long timescale for an introductory award, it formed part of the transfer strategy, and it was clear from the examples submitted in the assignments that the learning was being positively implemented across the business.

A further group has now gone through the programme with a similar level of success, Organisation E is addressing its future talent management challenges and is now offering the programme with a few minor alterations to people who they perceive as tomorrow's managers and leaders.

Organisation F

Participants reacted very well to the programme, so no specific changes were proposed to the format or content of the programme. However a number of areas were identified that would have improved the effectiveness of the programme and the ease of capturing ROI.

Participants' line managers must be willing and able to:

- Provide opportunities for participants to change
- Provide flexibility to try out new approaches
- Provide support to help embed their new learning
- Provide time and support to encourage completing the qualification

Increased emphasis needs to be placed on identifying barriers to applying the learning within the work place at the outset, as some managers stated they were unable to apply their learning to the workplace environment.

The self evaluation for each participant shows some positive and some disappointing information. Only four of the twelve participants completed the questionnaire before and after the programme. This level of response by the participants to the questionnaires demonstrates clearly the culture described by Darling (see page 17). We believe this was due to a lack of understanding of the process and a perception that the workshops were the cornerstone of the programme rather than just one part of the learning process. One of the key issues impacting upon this group of learners was the constantly changing structures and targets within the NHS which adds additional work pressures and can lead to a negative effect on morale.

Programme aims need to be more specific and measurable. Converting goals to cash is easier if the monetary value of some of these points is known at the outset. It is helpful where programme aims have metrics attached to them. Alternatively nationally accepted notional data and/or average hourly rates could be used to calculate efficiencies or time saved.

The low rate of completion of the award was a disappointment to us. Our experience in Organisations A and Organisation E gave us a high completion rate of coursework (85%). Completion here was actively encouraged by the Senior Management Teams, which motivated the learners. We now recommend to all our customers that if accredited programmes are chosen, then the qualification should be seen as a mandatory part of the learning programme.

Organisation G

Developing a culture change programme needs to be very carefully planned and should involve a number of champions and stakeholders to ensure a smooth implementation process.

Line managers need to be encouraged to provide practical opportunities to apply the new learning and remain open to new approaches from below.

The process gained momentum as it began to filter down into the organisation.

Teach the participants that the results will not be seen overnight, but they will see a gradual shift in approach.

Persisting with capturing ROI data has shown that this programme can pay for itself from savings made.

Organisation H

The NHS is a very challenging place for managers to work. The mix of external and internal change, coupled with many geographical bases, different populations and a hugely diverse staff mix adds to the complexity. The level of change that we have observed within the sector is at times bewildering and the sector seems to be in a constant of flux.

Each participant selected personal targets to work towards and each needed different types of support from their coach. With this type of programme, we recognise that group results may be less important than progress against individual benchmark and targets.

The level of line management support is recognised as a weakness, so in subsequent coaching cohorts we have introduced a joint coaching session with the line manager and participant present. This is designed to explore how the line manager can support the individual during the coaching programme. This has had some success although it has been difficult to track down more senior managers whose schedules appear to be fairly unmanageable.

Line managers will be encouraged to arrange three monthly sessions to review the goal setting progress and all coachees are expected to complete pre and post work around the 360° and profiling questionnaires. With future programmes, line managers will now attend session three which should increase their understanding and engagement levels.

We need to encourage coachees to think about return on investment and how some of their achievements can return cash savings or increased revenue to the business.

CHAPTER 13

TACKLING YOUR ROI CHALLENGE

This chapter explains the key steps required to enable organisations to solve their ROI challenge. Our experience is that you should tackle this in a number of phases and we recommend the following approach:

Conduct a climate review

We use a template to assess the Learning and Development climate and establish how conducive it is to managing ROI. We have set out below a typical set of questions / measures:

Organisational issues	What do we need to know?
Learning and development policy	What message does it convey? What level of compliance can be demonstrated across the organisation?
Advisory and or regulatory reports e.g. Investors in People, National Training Awards, Times Top 100, etc	What do they say about the Learning and Development approach? What suggestions have been made? Who takes responsibility for action?
What Learning and Development interventions does the organisation implement and what results data exists?	Training days per employee Off-the-job training days Training spend as a % of salary bill Proportion of staff with personal development plans Evaluation reports?
Profiling, assessment tools used	What currently exists? How are the results used for benchmarking and assessment processes?
How effectively is the	Organisational skills profile

functional capability of the workforce being developed?	Organisational qualifications profile Proportion of staff deemed at acceptable level of competence or above Proportion of employed and contract staff
How well are learning interventions supporting our critical success factors?	Types of learning and development available Level of take-up Does the learning and development affect the organisational key performance indicators? What are the expectations of learners? How well is the contribution to the bottom line understood? Do managers understand the contribution of learning to the success of the organisation?
Performance management	Does the Performance Review /Appraisal process clearly drive development? Does everyone have a Personal Development Plan? Does this link to organisational objectives? How skilled are appraisers, how well prepared are appraisees?
How does the investment in learning compare with that of other comparable organisations?	Spend on learning and development compared with relevant benchmark data about comparable organisations
Capture of tangible and intangible results	How is data currently collected? How are results communicated throughout the organisation?

Begin work with a small and receptive group

Introducing new ways of working is not easy and can result in a level of resistance. We have learned that it is better to begin with a receptive group who recognise the failings in the traditional approach. You will need to take the group through the Performance Improvement Cycle© and agree timescales and what the process will look like.

Once the process is underway it is important to circulate the results of any interventions across the organisation. This will increase the interest levels and engage others in the new process. At this stage it will prove easier to encourage others to adopt the new process and the engagement levels will be higher.

Changing the thinking of key stakeholders

It cannot be left to Learning and Development professionals to change the approach to learning within their organisation. There are five other key stakeholders involved in shaping the organisational climate and we believe the approach these currently take is listed in the middle column below.

This view was validated by over 100 participants at the CIPD Annual Conference November 2009. (Taggart 2009)[xxv]The trainer fights back: Happy sheet revenge.

Stakeholder	Today	Tomorrow
Chief Executive	Survival & talent identification	Growth & talent development
Finance Director	Cost	Profit/surplus
HR Director	Faith based	Evidence based
Line Manager	Detached	Engaged
Learner	Personal	Shared

It is, however, the role of Learning and Development professionals to help shift the approach to that shown on the far right. When stakeholders understand the importance of evaluating the outcomes from development initiatives, it helps to change the perception of development from a cost to an investment.

Key steps to developing a Return on Investment Culture

Evaluation, Benchmarking and Targets

- Corporate key performance indicators and organisational objectives should be transparent, and all development activities within an organisation should be clearly linked to these. Programme objectives should reflect these, so that all participants can align their own development activity to the organisation's drivers.

- The culture of the organisation should encourage continuous measurement by the use of benchmarking tools such as competency frameworks, 360° evaluations, performance audits etc.

Intervention and Transfer

- A strong champion is needed who has personal credibility and commitment to drive transfer strategies.
- The design of development programmes should be aligned with the company objectives to ensure they can be achieved.
- Using validation or accreditation delivers embedded learning.
- Using goals and projects demonstrates key impacts and improvements to working practice.
- Managers must understand that it is their job to support the development activities undertaken by their staff, incorporating a development discussion before and after training, helping individuals to set and review objectives, and identify opportunities to apply new processes. Compliance to this is vitally important to achieving embedded learning.
- Programme participants need to understand that more is expected of them than just attending learning events. Traditionally only the trainer is held accountable for performance. We recommend that both trainer and learner are evaluated, a significant change which needs to be introduced sensitively.
- The organisation needs to develop a range of learning transfer strategies which might include projects, goal setting, qualifications, study support, action learning and reflective practice.

Measurement and Return on Investment

The organisation needs to publicise metrics and details on its costs to help participants identify how and where their actions can make savings or increase revenue to improve the Return on Investment.

- Initial programme aims need to be more specific and measurable. Converting goals to cash is easier if the monetary value of some of these points are known at the outset.
- If ROI is your driver, programmes need to have metrics attached.
- If ROI is not the key driver intangible outputs will suffice, but these need to be identified at the start of the programme.
- ROI reports need to be circulated widely to show the impact that L&D is having on the performance of the business. This teaches employees to think about the bottom line and their contribution to it.

Return on Investment made easier!

Our experience has proven that the Performance Improvement Cycle© helps organisations to improve their approach to Learning and Development and produces positive ROI results. In its current form however it can be resource intensive and thus can limit the scope to apply it on a large scale. This is a source of frustration to us especially when we consider the savings and benefits it has delivered to our customers. It is very clear to us that the way forward is to automate our PIC© into a web based system and then offer this to our customers on a sale or licence basis.

We have spent the last 6 years refining our PIC© and are now very confident that our system is ready to be fully automated. This will facilitate the transformation that we are promoting around organisational learning and allow organisations to self manage this transformation.

Our research has included visiting Return on Investment and HR software conferences in the USA and UK to view current systems. Most systems are electronic record keeping and course booking systems, e-learning systems or modular OD systems. This highlights the fragmented nature of L&D systems, which we believe serves to confuse the L&D professional in their search for an effective system. Few, if any of these systems deal with the important issues of learning transfer or produce ROI reports.

Odissy™ which stands for Organisational Development Improvement Software SYstem is a holistic and user friendly web based software system that will transform the learning and development function from a cost centre to a profit centre. It will manage ROI, all learning programmes, automate talent management, succession planning and performance management processes and plug the gaps missing in current systems.

Odissy™ allows an organisation to measure the impact of all development interventions and produces reports that can be used for a range of purposes including board reports,

Investor in People evidence and National Training Award Submissions. The reports can be used to identify successful programmes and improve or scrap the less successful ones. This will stop customers spending money on interventions that deliver a limited or no ROI.

Benefits for all

- Executives will love Odissy™ as it will demonstrate that the L&D investment is improving the performance of the organisation

- Managers will love Odissy™ as their results will improve through having a more skilled and effective workforce

- Employees will love Odissy™ as it will improve their promotion opportunities, appraisal ratings and pay progression through a more effective application and reporting of new skills and learning

- L&D professionals will love Odissy™ as it will transform the perception of their function from a cost centre to a profit centre

For more information visit the website www.odissy.co.uk or contact us at GPSVision Ltd.

We have set out below a typical Programme Report that Odissy™ will generate from data entered by managers who have engaged in a leadership programme. Reports can be produced by development programme, by employee, by department and at organisational level.

odissy®

revolutionising organisational development

Firework Frenzy

Leadership Practice Cohort

Programme Report

17th February 2010

Introduction

This report provides data against 9 areas. The first 4 areas set out the company and programme objectives, programme costs and who engaged in the programme. The final 5 areas show the results against five measures. The outputs have been gathered at a number of intervals during the programme.

1. Company Objectives
2. Programme Objectives
3. Programme Costs
4. Who was registered for the programme?
5. How did people find the session?
6. Did they learn anything?
7. Did they change their behaviour?
8. What was the impact?
9. Monetary Return on Investment

1. Company Objectives

TYPE	Organisation
MEASURE	Profitability
INDUSTRY BENCHMARK	25%
EXISTING INFORMATION	10%
ISSUES / PROBLEMS	Too low
TARGET FOR IMPROVEMENT	15%
EVIDENCE TO BE CITED	Annual accounts

TYPE	Staff and Team
MEASURE	Staff Turnover
INDUSTRY BENCHMARK	N/A
EXISTING INFORMATION	21%
ISSUES / PROBLEMS	Too high due to poor supervisory skills
TARGET FOR IMPROVEMENT	10%
EVIDENCE TO BE CITED	HR statistics

TYPE	Staff and Team
MEASURE	Absence figures
INDUSTRY BENCHMARK	N/A
EXISTING INFORMATION	15%
ISSUES / PROBLEMS	Too high due to poor morale
TARGET FOR IMPROVEMENT	10%
EVIDENCE TO BE CITED	Staff survey and absence figures

2. Programme Objectives

	TYPE	MEASURE	INDUSTRY BENCHMARK	EXISTING INFO	ISSUES / PROBLEMS	TARGET	EVIDENCE
1	Organisation	Profitability	N/A	£300,000	Need to increase customer base	350,000	Financial figures
2	Staff and Team	PDM Results	N/A	70% of PDR's were completed last year	skills of managers and commitment	90% of PDR's should be completed next year	HR statistics

3. Programme Costs

Staff Costs	
Room Costs	£1000
Material Costs	£200
Trainer Costs	£3000
Programme Costs	£2400
Registration Costs	£600

4. Who was registered for the programme?

Andy Allsopp Steven Sedgwick Harriet Hair Susan Styles

Attendance

EVENT NAME	DATE OF EVENT	NO. ATTENDED	NO. ABSENT
Induction session	10/11/2009	3	1
Workshop 1	17/11/2009	3	1
Workshop 2	18/12/2009	3	1
Workshop 3	24/01/2010	2	2

5. How did people find the session?

Average feedback scores. Key 5 = excellent 1 = poor

Workshop Summary

How valuable was the workshop for your current role?	3.5
Were you happy with the content?	3.5
How much did you enjoy the workshop?	4
How did you rate the trainers?	4.25
Will you be able to use the learning in your own workplace?	3.5

6. Did the group learn anything?

Workshop Summary

Assignment description	no. passed	no. outstanding	no. failed / not submitted
Leadership practice assignment	4	0	0

7. Did the group change their behaviour?

Questionnaire Results

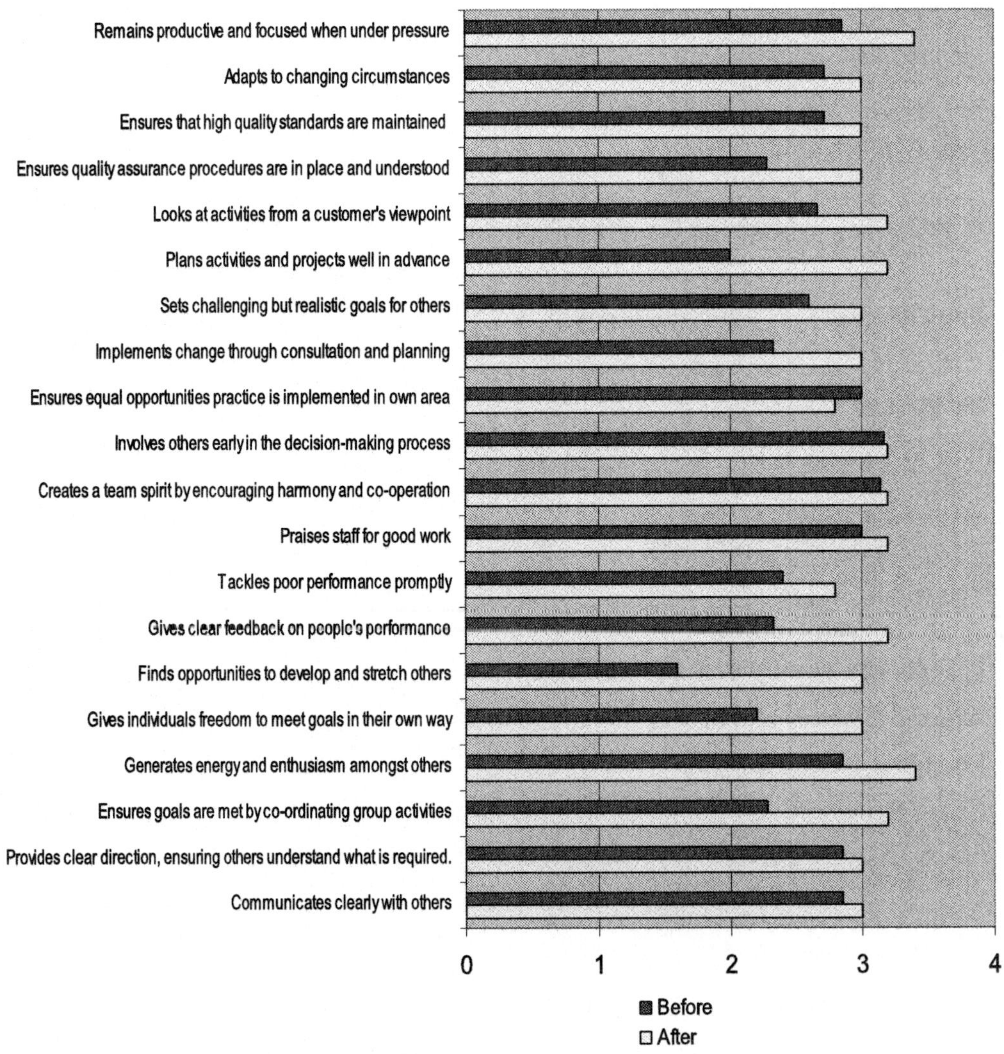

Goals and Projects Summary

	Number set	Number completed	Number outstanding	Number overdue
GOALS	5	4	1	0
PROJECTS	3	3	0	0

8. What was the impact?

Goals

GOAL NAME	ROI VALUE(GBP)	ROI IMPACT
Complete PDR's	5,000	All staff are focused on achieving their business objectives which has improved organisational sales performance by 10%
Newsletter contribution	0	Raise profile of the team
Profitability increase team sales	250	1% increase on team sales
New team meeting structure	3,000	Saved one hour per week per person

Projects

PROJECT NAME	ROI VALUE(GBP)	ROI IMPACT
New changeover process	10,000	A reduction of 10% in changeover time has resulted in £10,000 savings
Improved Sales figures	20,000	Increased sales volume at current costs has increased revenue by £20,000
Software Services	10,000	The new software implementation has produced £10,000 new sales

9. Return on Investment

$$\frac{\text{Benefit from training} - \text{cost of training} \times 100}{\text{Cost of training}} = \text{ROI\%}$$

$$\frac{£48250 - £7200 \times 100}{£7200} = 570\%$$

REFERENCES AND FURTHER READING

References

i ASTD Research Talent Management, Practices and Opportunities, 2008,

ii Saratoga/Pricewaterhouse Coopers Key trends in human capital: a Global perspective 2005,

iii Kearns, P Evaluating the ROI from Learning. London : CIPD, 2005

iv Chartered Management Institute Talent management - Maximising talent for Business Performance, Nov 2007

v Saratoga/Pricewaterhouse Coopers 2005

vi 2005 Leadership Forecast DDI People Management June 2005

vii GPSVision White Paper Paradigm shift in Leadership Development 2005

viii DDI Survey Report 2008

ix Why is ROI controversial? White paper Knowledge Advisors 2009

x Kirkpatrick D, Evaluating Training Programs Berrett-Koehler, 1994.

xi Phillips Jack J Return on Investment in Training and Performance Improvement Programs Butterworth-Heinemann, 2003

xii Darling J www.performance_knowledge.com 2006

xiii Holton, E. F. III, Bates, R. A., & Ruona, W. E. A. Development of a Generalized Learning Transfer System Inventory. 2000

xiv Kearns, P 2005

xv Bennis, W, Leadership Institute of University of Southern California, ' Ways to instil those illusive qualities, Financial Times, Nov, 2005

xvi GPSVision White Paper, Paradigm Shift

xvii Apter International Eight ways of being diagnostic guide

xviii Darling J 2006

xix Pedler, M., Burgoyne, J. and Boydell, T. The Learning Company. A strategy for sustainable development, London: McGraw-Hill. 1991, 1996

xx Senge, P. et. al. The Fifth Discipline Fieldbook: Strategies and Tools for Building a Learning Organization 1994

xxi Kaoru Ishikawa Introduction to Quality Control Springer 1991

xxii De Bono Six Thinking Hats Penguin 2004

xxiii Lewin K Field Theory in Social Science 1951Harper and Row, New York

xxiv Apter International www.apterinternational.com

xxv Taggart P The Trainer fights back: Happy Sheet revenge CIPD conference presentation 2009

Further Reading

Boyatzis R, (2005)Leadership Financial Times August

CIPD, (2004) Helping people learn Research Report

Cranet Survey, http://www.cranet.org/about/about.htm

DDI (2005) People Management, Leadership Forecast

Groot, W (1999) Productivity Effects of Enterprise Related Training Applied Economic Letters, vol 6, pp 369-71

Haskel, J, Hawkes D, May (2003) Office of National Statistics

IFS (2004) Working Paper No. W00/04, Training and Corporate Productivity in a Panel of British Industries, March.

Kirkpatrick, J (2005) Transferring learning to behaviour' ASTD,

Kuhn, Thomas, S. (1970) "The Structure of Scientific Revolutions", Second Edition, University of Chicago Press, Chicago,

Lynch, Lisa and Sandra Black (1995) Beyond the Incidence of Training: Evidence from a National Employers Survey National Bureau of Economic Research Working Paper No. 5231, Cambridge, Massachusetts.

Patterson M, West M A, Lawthom R, Nickell S (1998) Impact of People Management Practices on Business Performance, IPD, London

Schuster, F. E. (1986) The Schuster Report: The Proven Connection Between People and Profit, New York: Wiley.